He Shall Glorify Me

Talks on the Holy Spirit and other themes

by
Oswald Chambers

DISTRIBUTORS:

SIMPKIN MARSHALL (1941), LTD.

ROSSMORE COURT, PARK ROAD, LONDON, N.W.1

These verbatim notes were first published in the "B.T.C. Monthly Journal."

Reprinted 1949

Made and Printed in Great Britain by
Butler & Tanner Ltd., Frome and London

CONTENTS

FOREWORD

It is my privilege to have been asked to write a brief Foreword to this book, the latest addition to the treasure-house of the Oswald Chambers literature. The idea of a Foreword is surely that some fact may be brought to light, the telling of which shall induce others to read and so share in the life-giving truth.

The writer enjoyed a close friendship with 'O. C.', and there came to his own life fresh spiritual impetus and vision as he not only listened to the exposition of truths, but as he saw those same truths practised and lived out in everyday contact with men and affairs. It was indeed a life lived in abandon to God.

The whole story of the 'O. C.' literature is an outstanding witness of the gracious hand of God. Oswald Chambers spent the last two years of his life in Y.M.C.A. work out in the desert in Egypt, in the thick of it with the men, every evening being devoted to a meeting for spiritual instruction on some vital theme. This book in particular is compiled largely from these talks, as well as from sermons delivered on Sundays. Then in November 1917 came his Home-call into God's immediate presence, and a leaflet was printed and scattered among the men in Egypt and Palestine in time for Christmas. There was little thought at the time of the number of books to which this leaflet, entitled 'The Place of Help', was to be the forerunner. Other publications quickly began to follow, and each one was printed simultaneously in Egypt and in England. I have had the joy and privilege of being associated with the publishing from those early days right on until now; and with the growing demand for all the books, and for their translation into a number of languages, one feels confident that God will unfold yet more of His purpose in this great work.

So read and study and enjoy this new book, and find for yourself that 'The Best is yet to be', as 'O. C.' so frequently reminded us.

Dunstable.   P. W. L.

7

THE ADVENT OF THE HOLY SPIRIT

"Howbeit when He, the Spirit of truth, is come, . . . He shall glorify Me" (John xvi. 13–14).

There are two descents of the Holy Spirit mentioned in the Bible: the first is at the baptism of our Lord, the second on the Day of Pentecost, when the Paraclete came to this earth. The power of the Holy Spirit and His personal presence are not the same; the power of the Holy Spirit was mightily present in the world before His personal advent. In this dispensation we not only have the power of the Holy Spirit, but His personal presence moving amongst us.

THE PEACE OF GOD.

"And the Holy Spirit descended in a bodily shape like a dove upon Him, and a voice from heaven, which said, Thou art My beloved Son; in Thee I am well pleased" (Luke iii. 22).

The first descent of the Holy Spirit was upon the Son of Man—that is, the whole human race represented in one Person, and that Person the historic Jesus Christ who was God Incarnate. It was at His baptism that the Holy Spirit descended upon Him, and we must never forget that His baptism was a baptism of repentance. It was at His baptism that Jesus Christ definitely took upon Him His vocation, which was to bear away the sin of the world.

John the Baptist must not be regarded as a mere individual; Jesus said of him that he was the greatest prophet that had been born of woman, and he is the last of the line of prophets. After four hundred years of absolute silence there came this lonely, mighty voice, 'Prepare . . .' Jesus said to John, "for thus it becometh us to fulfil all righteousness." That could only be done by Our Lord as the Son of man accepting His vocation to bear away the sin of the world. Jesus is the 'Prince of Peace' because only in Him can men have God's

9   A*

good-will and peace on earth. Thank God, through that beloved Son the great peace of God may come to every heart and to every nation under heaven, but it can come in no other way. None of us can ever have good-will towards God if we won't listen to His Son. Have we despised what the Father said about Jesus Christ at His baptism? On the Mount of Transfiguration He said the same thing. The only way to peace and salvation and power, and to all that God has in the way of benedictions and blessings for us individually and for the whole world, is in the Son of Man.

The Power of God.

"And there appeared unto them cloven tongues like as of fire," (Acts ii. 3).

The second mighty descent of the Holy Spirit was on the Day of Pentecost, when the power of God came in Person. The record says that they who heard were devout Jews from every nation under heaven, and the great miracle is stated—"how hear we every man in our own tongue?" The Holy Spirit came not as a dove, but in cloven tongues of fire. The disciples had been told to tarry until they were endued with power from on high. As soon as Jesus Christ was glorified, the personal Holy Spirit descended, and in the decrees of God the fulness of time was reached when the Son of Man, on whom the Holy Spirit had descended as a dove, ascended to the right hand of the Father and sent forth the mighty Holy Spirit. In Genesis v. we read that God caused confusion of tongues; on the Day of Pentecost He caused a fusion of understanding by the tongues of fire, the manifestation accompanying the personal advent of the Holy Spirit. It was a far-reaching, mighty testimony to the fact that sin had been judged on the Cross.

It is one thing to believe that the Holy Spirit is given individually, but another thing to receive the revelation that He is here. He is here in personal presence in all the plenitude of His power, but His power will only work as a manifestation of what Jesus Christ has done. The Holy Spirit

10

works in no other way than to glorify Jesus Christ. Anyone who receives the Holy Spirit receives life from the glorified Jesus, and receives also an understanding of the teaching of Jesus and complete security, provided he abides in the light the Holy Spirit sheds.

"Verily, verily, I say unto you, He that believeth on Me, the works that I do shall he do also; and greater works than these shall he do; because I go unto my Father." (John xiv. 12.) It was this mighty Person, the Holy Spirit, who inspired the apostles to write the New Testament. The New Testament is the posthumous writing of Jesus Christ; He departed, and the Holy Spirit used these men as His pens to expound His teaching.

THE PATIENCE OF GOD.

"For by one Spirit are we all baptized into one body" (1 Corinthians xii. 13).

The baptism of the Holy Spirit delivers us from independent individuality. The one thing the Holy Spirit awakens and brings into communion with God is what is meant by personality. Individual self-assertiveness is the husk, personal identity with the Lord is the kernel. The Holy Spirit builds us into the Body of Christ.

All that Jesus Christ came to do is made experimentally ours by the Holy Spirit; He does *in* us what Jesus did *for* us. The gifts of the Spirit are not for individual exaltation, but for the good of the whole Body of Christ. The Body of Christ is an organism, not an organization. How patient God is in forming the Body of Christ.

Our Lord's words in John xvi. 14 sum up the personal passion of the Holy Spirit, "He shall glorify Me." The word 'passion' has come down in the world; it is generally taken to mean a distemper from which human nature suffers, but when the phrase "the Passion of our Lord" is used it means the transfiguration of peace and power and patience.

THE DOCTRINE OF THE
HOLY SPIRIT—I

(I.) "The Beyond. that is Within."

"Verily, verily, I say unto thee, Except a man be born again, he cannot see the kingdom of God" (John iii. 3).

This title * will serve as a comment on Our Lord's words to Nicodemus. The power to see is within; what is seen is without, otherwise it is hallucination. When the Holy Spirit comes in there is a new power of perception—"And their eyes were opened, and they knew Him;" "Then opened He their understanding, that they might understand the scriptures." (Luke xxiv. 31, 45.) The Holy Spirit regenerates my personal spirit, that is, I receive a quickening life which puts the 'beyond' within, and immediately the 'beyond' has come within it rises up to the 'above', and I enter the domain where Jesus lives.

"Nicodemus saith unto Him, How can a man be born when he is old?" Nicodemus's question was not captious, it was a sensible, profound question arising out of the tremendously sweeping statement Jesus had made—"Except a man be born again, he cannot see the kingdom of God." The phrase "born again" was not new to Nicodemus, for the Rabbis spoke of a convert from heathenism as being 'born again'; but the application Jesus made of it was absolutely amazing. "Marvel not that I said unto thee, Ye must be" —not developed, not educated, but "born again"—'fundamentally made all over again, before you can see the kingdom of God and enter into it.'

Remember, Jesus is not talking to one whom men would call a sinner, there is no mention of sin; He is talking to a religious man, to "the teacher of Israel"; it is to him Jesus says, "Ye must be born again." If you define sin as external wrong doing, you miss out this class of men, men like the

* *"The Beyond that is Within,"* by E. Boutroux.

12

rich young ruler ("Master, all these have I observed from my youth"); men like Saul of Tarsus ("touching the righteousness which is in the law, blameless")—men who do not need saving from external wrong doing, they are not guilty of any. Talk about "Broken Earthenware", about going to the slums to save men and women, and every one's sympathy is with you; but Nicodemus was not 'broken earthenware', he was not an outcast of society; he was a cultured Pharisee, an honoured member of the Sanhedrim, and here stands a young Nazarene Carpenter and says to him, quietly and calmly, "Ye must be born again." No wonder Nicodemus was absolutely bewildered—'I can understand how by education, religious and otherwise, I can make myself a little better; how by careful training I can keep out of sight the ugly things in my disposition; but what you say about being made all over again, I cannot understand at all.'

Jesus Christ's salvation deals not only with the outcast and downtrodden, it deals with clean-living, upright, sterling men and women, and immediately you present the Gospel as Jesus presents it, it is this class you clash with. Jesus Christ came to do what no man can do for himself, viz., alter his disposition. "How can a man be born when he is old?" By receiving the gift of the Holy Spirit, and allowing Him to do *in* him what Jesus did *for* him. The mighty sovereign power of God can re-make a man from within and readjust him to God. The Holy Spirit is God Himself working to make the Redemption efficacious in human lives. No wonder men leap for joy when they get saved in the New Testament way!

"Marvel not that I said unto thee, Ye must be born again." Our Lord is talking about a momentous practical experience, viz., being born from above while we live in the below. The conception of new birth in the New Testament is not of something that springs out of us, what modern psychology calls 'a subliminal uprush', but of something that comes into us. Just as Our Lord came into the world from the outside, so He must come into us from the outside. The "washing of regeneration" comes consciously to our personal lives in

13

and through the words of the New Testament—". . . being born again, . . . by the word of God" (1 Peter i. 23). There is no authentic impulse of the Holy Spirit that is not wedded to the words of the Bible. To recognize this is the only way to be safe from dangerous delusions. To-day our beliefs are being rationalized, men are denying the supernatural element, that the Spirit of God comes in and does something which transcends human reason. A Christian is an impossible being unless a man can be made all over again. Everything hangs on this one central statement of Jesus— "*Ye must be born again.*" We have lost sight of it, and we have got to get back to it.

(II.) THE WITHIN THAT IS ABOVE.

"If thou knewest the gift of God, and who it is that saith to thee, Give Me to drink; thou wouldest have asked of Him, and He would have given thee living water" (John iv. 10).

The idea of receiving anything as a gift from God is staggeringly original; we imagine we have to earn things by prayer and obedience. We cannot earn or win anything from God, we must receive it as a gift, like a pauper, or do without it. In this verse Our Lord is describing the essential nature of the gift—"He would have given thee living water" —a living, amazing reality. There is nothing profounder in the whole of the New Testament than this interview, it is full of the great meaning of the Gospel of God; we do not sufficiently grasp its profundity. In it we see Almighty God Incarnate stooping down to lift up a sinful woman, as a symbol of the way His salvation is at work among men.

Our Lord did not use means to attract the woman, she happened to be there—"and He must needs go through Samaria". Watch the method of His procedure, it is amazing. Our Lord does not begin by telling the woman she is a sinner, He begins by asking her to give Him something—"Give Me to drink." There is no condescension in grace, a sinner is never afraid of Jesus; the Pharisees hated Him, that is why He said to them—"Verily I say unto you, That the

14

publicans and the harlots flock into the kingdom of God before you." (Matthew xxi. 31.) The woman was surprised at His request, not because of His personality, but because of His nationality, it was a perplexity on the surface of things. "How is it that Thou, being a Jew, askest drink of me, which am a woman of Samaria? for the Jews have no dealings with the Samaritans." "Thou, being a Jew" . . .; "a woman of Samaria"—both titles were absurdly insufficient. In the sight of God the woman is representative of the whole world—Jesus Christ is Almighty God Incarnate.

"If thou knewest the gift of God, . . . He would have given thee living water." The Gift of God is the Son of God; the gift from the Gift of God is the Holy Spirit. Jesus did not talk about "the gift of God" to the Master of Israel; to him He talked about the need to be born again; He talked about the gift of God to a poor, ignorant, sinful woman. To her He did not say, "Ye must be born again"; He spoke of a gift which would regenerate her, i.e., become in her "a well of water springing up into everlasting life." Our Lord gave the exposition of His salvation, not to Nicodemus, a man of sterling character, but to a sinful woman, and she understood without knowing that she did. She was plainly confused, and yet she trusted Him and asked for the gift, "Sir, give me this water . . ." Instantly reproof followed on her request. (vv. 16–18.) That is always the method of the Holy Spirit; we usurp the place of the Holy Spirit when we try to convict a man of sin first.

Our Lord never talked in stages of experience, that is, He does not talk to our heads, He instructs us in our relationship to Himself. Here, He is leading a woman into the grace of God; the overflowing favour of God, it is so overflowing that we trample it under foot; it seems so humble and gentle that we ignore it. Jesus is dealing with the grace of God towards sinners, and the characteristic of the grace of God is that it wells up into everlasting life, "a fountain of living water"—not merely a clean heart, but a full one, being kept clean.

THE DOCTRINE OF THE HOLY SPIRIT—II

The Bounty of Destitution

John vii. 37-39

Generally speaking, Our Lord does not deal with the experimental stages of salvation, He deals with the great revelation facts; the Holy Spirit expounds the experimental stages. Our Lord makes no divisions such as conversion, regeneration, sanctification, He presents the truth in nugget form and the apostles beat out the nuggets into negotiable gold, it is in their writings that we have the stages of experience worked out. Always view the Epistles as the posthumous work of the ascended Christ; don't say, 'That is only what Paul says.' In the Epistles we have not got Paul's ideas or Peter's ideas; we have the ideas of the Holy Ghost, and the 'pens' happen to be Paul or Peter or John. ". . . holy men of God spake as they were moved by the Holy Ghost" (2 Peter i. 21).

(I.) Christ's Infinite Patience and Human Destitution

"In the last day, the great day of the feast, Jesus stood and cried saying, If any man thirst, let him come unto Me, and drink" (v. 37).

Our Lord begins where we would never begin, at the point of human destitution. The greatest blessing a man ever gets from God is the realization that if he is going to enter into His Kingdom it must be through the door of destitution. Naturally we do not want to begin there, that is why the appeal of Jesus is of no use until we come face to face with realities; then the only One worth listening to is the Lord. We learn to welcome the patience of Jesus only when we get to the point of human destitution. It is not that God *will not* do anything for us until we get there, but that He *cannot*. God can do nothing for me if I am sufficient for myself. When we come to the place of destitution spiritually we find the Lord waiting, and saying, "If any man thirst, let him come unto Me, and drink." There are hundreds at the place of destitution and they don't know what they want. If I have been obeying the command of Jesus to 'go and make disciples,' I know what they want; they want Him. We are so interested in our own spiritual riches that souls that are white unto harvest are all around us and we don't reap one for Him.

Some men enter the Kingdom of heaven through crushing, tragic, overwhelming conviction of sin, but they are not the greatest number; the greatest number enter the Kingdom along this line of spiritual destitution—no power to lay hold of God, no power to do what I ought to do, utterly poverty-stricken. Then, says Jesus, blessed are you, because you have come to the place where you can receive the gift of the Holy Spirit. We are told by some that it is foolish to tell people to ask for the Holy Spirit because this is the dispensation of the Holy Spirit. Thank God it is! God's mighty Spirit is with all men, He impinges on their lives at all points and in unexpected ways, but the great need is to receive the Holy Spirit. There stands the promise for every one who will put it to the test: "If ye then, being evil, know how to give good gifts to your children: how much more shall your heavenly Father give the Holy Spirit to them that ask Him?" The bedrock in Jesus Christ's kingdom is poverty, not possession; not decisions for Christ, but a sense of absolute futility—'I can't begin to do it.' That is the entrance; and it does take us a long while to believe we are poor. It is at the point of destitution that the bounty of God can be given.

(II.) CHRIST'S INFINITE PROMISE AND HUMAN DEPENDENCE.

"He that believeth on Me, as the Scripture hath said, out of him shall flow rivers of living water" (v. 38).

To the woman of Samaria, Jesus talked of the benefits to the individual personal life of the living water—"the water that I shall give him shall become in him a well of water springing up into eternal life" (ch. iv. 14). Here, He is talking not of the benefits to the individual life at all, but of the rivers of living water that will flow out of the individual life. Jesus did not say, 'He that believeth on Me, shall experience the fulness of the blessing of God'; but, 'he that believeth on Me, out of him shall escape everything he receives.' It is a picture of the unfathomable, incalculable benediction which will flow from the one great sovereign source, belief in Jesus. We have nothing to do with the outflow; we have to see to it that we are destitute enough of spiritual independence to be filled with the Holy Ghost and then pay attention to the Source, Our Lord Himself. You can never measure what God will do through you if you are rightly related to Jesus. The parenthesis in *v.* 39 does not apply to us: the Holy Ghost *has been* given; Jesus *is* glorified; the rivers of living water are there, and, unspeakable wonder! the sacrament may flow through our lives too. All that the one out of whom the rivers of living water are flowing is conscious of is belief in Jesus and maintaining a right relationship to Him; then day by day God is pouring the rivers of living water through you, and it is of His mercy He does not let you know it.

(III.) CHRIST'S INFINITE POWER AND HUMAN DEVOTION.

"(But this spake He of the Spirit, which they that believe on Him should receive: for the Holy Ghost was not yet given; because that Jesus was not yet glorified)" (*v.* 39).

The abiding vital meaning of Pentecost is not that "there were added unto them about three thousand souls"; what happened at Pentecost was that Our Lord was glorified, and that He shed forth from above the Holy Ghost in the plentitude of His power. "Therefore being by the right hand of God exalted, and having received of the Father the promise of the Holy Ghost, He hath shed forth this, which ye now see and hear" (Acts ii. 33). The gift of the Holy Spirit is the impartation of a personal Spirit that blends the

18

historic Son of God and the individual believer into one, and the characteristic of the life is devotion to God, so much so that you don't even know you are devoted to Him until a crisis comes. When you have become united to Jesus it is impossible to talk about your experiences or to pray for yourself because you have been brought into a oneness with Him even as He was one with the Father. The 'Higher Christian Life' type of teaching is apt to lead us not to worshipping God and to being devoted to Jesus, but merely to pietistic experiences. The snare of experiences is that we keep coming back to the shore when God wants to get us out into the deeps. The one great thing about the salvation of Jesus is that the more you experience it the less you know what you experience; it is only in the initial stages that you know what you experience. The danger is lest we mistake the shores of our experience for the ocean. The experimental aspect of the baptism of the Holy Ghost is not defined by the historic Pentecost, but by Our Lord's words in Acts i. 8—"But ye shall receive power, after that the Holy Ghost is come upon you: and ye shall be *witnesses unto Me.*" The spirit that comes in is not that of doing anything for Jesus, but of being a perfect delight to Him.

THE DOCTRINE OF THE
HOLY SPIRIT—III

THE GREATEST DAY YET

"And when the day of Pentecost was now come, . . ."
("was being fulfilled," R.V. marg., Acts ii. 1).

What an unspeakably wonderful day the Day of Pentecost was! There is only one Bethlehem, one Calvary, one Pentecost; these are the landmarks of Time and Eternity, everything and everyone is judged by them.

Beware of thinking of Pentecost in the light of personal experience only. The descent of the Holy Ghost can never be experimental, it is historical. The reception of the Holy Ghost into our hearts is experimental. Those who insist on the experimental line are in danger of forgetting the revelation and of putting all the emphasis on experience, while those who emphasize the revelation are in danger of forgetting the practical experience. In the New Testament the two are one; the experimental must be based on and regulated by the revelation. We imagine that we have the monopoly of the teaching about the Holy Spirit when we deal with His work in individual lives, viz., His power to transform men on the inside—the most important phase to us, but in God's Book the tiniest phase of the work of the mighty Spirit of God.

(I.) THE ACCOMPLISHMENT OF THE PROMISE OF THE SON.
(John xiv. 26, xv. 16, xvi. 7–15; cf. Matthew iii. 11.)

These verses are the testimony of Jesus to the Holy Ghost, whom He calls 'the Comforter', 'the Paraclete'. Our Lord told His disciples that it was expedient for them that He should go away because the Paraclete would not come until His work was completed. ". . . if I go, I will send Him unto you." We know the Holy Spirit first of all through the testimony of Jesus to Him, and then through the conscious enjoyment of His indwelling presence—"for He abideth with you, and shall be in you."

John xx. 22 (". . . He breathed on them, and saith unto them, Receive ye the Holy Ghost:") and Acts ii. 33 ("Being therefore by the right hand of God exalted, and having received of the Father the promise of the Holy Ghost, He hath poured forth this, which ye see and hear.") do not refer to the same thing. When Jesus breathed on the disciples what they received was the quickening of new life from the Risen Lord: Pentecost stands for something unrepeatable in the history of the world, viz., the personal descent of the Paraclete. The Holy Ghost came into this world on the Day of Pentecost, and He has been here ever since. He is here, but indiscernible, as Jesus was saving to the few who had the revelation that He was God Incarnate. Have we received the revelation of who the Holy Ghost is?

"Howbeit when He, the Spirit of truth is come, . . . He shall glorify Me." We lose the marvel of the indwelling of the Holy Spirit by thinking of Him as some power that does things. The most rarely recognized aspect of the Holy Spirit's work is that He causes us to do honour to Our Lord. The human spirit uninspired by the Holy Spirit only honours Jesus if He *does* things. It is easier to dishonour Jesus than we are apt to think because He never insists on being honoured. The Holy Ghost is the One who honours Jesus, and therein lies the essential necessity of receiving Him. "He shall glorify *Me,*" said Jesus. The Holy Spirit does not glorify Christ-likeness, because Christ-likeness can be imitated; He glorifies Christ. It is impossible to imitate Jesus Christ.

(II.) THE ACCOMPLISHMENT OF THE PROMISE OF THE FATHER.
    (Luke xxiv. 49; Acts i. 8.)

"And behold, I send forth the promise of My Father upon you."

Do you say 'I am waiting for my Pentecost'? Who told

21

you to wait? 'Oh, I am waiting as the disciples did in the upper room.' Not all the waiting on earth will ever gain you the baptism with the Holy Ghost. The baptism with the Holy Ghost is the infallible sign that Jesus has ascended to the right hand of God and has received of the Father the promise of the Holy Ghost. We too often divorce what the New Testament never divorces: the baptism with the Holy Ghost is not an experience apart from Christ, it is the evidence that He has ascended. It is not the baptism with the Holy Ghost that changes men, it is the power of the ascended Christ coming into men's lives by the Holy Ghost that changes them.

". . . but tarry ye in the city, until ye be clothed with power from on high." "Power from on high"—the words have a fascinating sound in the ears of men; but this power is not a magical power, not the power to work miracles; it is the power that transforms character, that sanctifies faculties. "But ye shall receive power, when the Holy Ghost is come upon you:" said Jesus to the disciples, and they did—the power that made them like their Lord. (cf. Acts iv. 13.) It is easy to have the idea that we receive the Holy Spirit as a sort of magical power all to ourselves; the reception of the Holy Spirit is for the purpose of quickening us into identification with Our Lord. We live in utter unadulterated loyalty to the Son of God by reason of the fact that we have received His testimony regarding the Holy Ghost and have received Him into our hearts. People come piously together and ask God to baptize them with the Holy Ghost, but they forget that the first thing the Holy Ghost does is to illuminate the Cross of Christ. The emphasis in the New Testament is always on the Cross. The Cross is the secret of the heart of God, the secret of the Person of the Son of God, the secret of the Holy Ghost's work. It is the Cross alone that made it possible for God to give us the gift of eternal life, and to usher in the great era in which we live— the dispensation of the Holy Ghost.

". . . and ye shall be My witnesses. The historic Pentecost made these men the incarnation of the Holy Ghost.

The apostles became 'written epistles', i.e., the expression of what they preached. When a man experiences salvation the note of testimony is what Jesus has done for him; when he is baptized with the Holy Ghost he becomes a witness, which means much more than a testifier to blessings received. A witness means that just as Jesus was made broken bread and poured-out wine for our salvation, so we are to be broken bread and poured-out wine in sacrificial service. The baptism with the Holy Ghost is Jesus putting the final seal on His work in you, His seal on your regenerated and entirely sanctified soul, and is your inauguration into service for Him. The Holy Spirit always works through human instrumentality, and there is never any possibility of pride when the Holy Spirit uses us. We are empowered into union with Christ by the Holy Ghost.

THE DOCTRINE OF THE HOLY SPIRIT—IV

THE SPIRIT'S CATHEDRAL

Ephesians ii. 19–22

(I.) THE HABITATION OF THE HOLY GHOST IN THE MORTAL CHRISTIAN.

"What? know ye not that your body is the temple of the Holy Ghost . . . ?" (1 Corinthians vi. 19).

It is one thing to have participated in regeneration and sanctification and quite another thing to enjoy the knowledge that your body is "the temple of the Holy Ghost". That is not an experience, it is a revelation, and a revelation which takes some believing, and then some obeying. Many even in the experience of entire sanctification are ignorant of what the Apostle Paul is talking about. As saints our brains ought to be used to systematize and make our own the great revelations given in God's word regarding His purpose for us. People say, 'I have received the Holy Spirit, therefore everything I want to do is inspired by Him.' By no means; I have to see that I instruct myself regarding these revelations which are only interpreted to me by the Holy Ghost, never by my natural wisdom. There are some saints who are ideally actual, i.e., instructed as well as sanctified and living in unsullied communion with God, and there are others who are like Ephraim, "a cake not turned". Once let it dawn on your mind that your body is the temple of the Holy Ghost and instantly the impossible becomes possible; the things you used to pray about, you no longer pray about, but *do*. As in the natural world, so in the spiritual, knowledge is power. All we need to *experience* is that we have "passed out of death into life": what we need to *know* takes all Time and Eternity. "And this is life eternal, that they might know Thee the only true God. . . ." (John xvii. 3.) Begin to know Him now, and finish never!

24

". . . in whom ye also are builded together for an habitation of God through the Spirit" (Ephesians ii. 19–22). The conception in these verses is wonderful in its illuminating power, viz. God is building us for Himself. He does not explain why He takes us certain ways, but this passage explains it: He is building a habitation for Himself.

> I am his house—for him to go in and out.
> He builds me now—and if I cannot see
> At any time what he is doing with me,
> 'Tis that he makes the house for me too grand.
> GEORGE MACDONALD.

(II.) THE HABITATION OF THE HOLY GHOST IN THE MYSTIC CHRIST.

"For by one Spirit are we all baptized into one body, . . ." (1 Corinthians xii. 13–27).

God is the Architect of the human body and He is also the Architect of the Body of Christ. There are two Bodies of Christ: the Historic Body and the Mystical Body. The historic Jesus was the habitation of the Holy Ghost (*see* Luke iii. 22; John i. 32–33), and the Mystic Christ, i.e., the Body of Christ composed of those who have experienced regeneration and sanctification, is likewise the habitation of the Holy Ghost. When we are baptized with the Holy Ghost we are no longer isolated believers but part of the Mystical Body of Christ. Beware of attempting to live a holy life alone, it is impossible. Paul continually insists on the 'together' aspect—"God hath quickened us *together*, . . . and hath raised us up *together*, and made us sit *together* . . ." (Ephesians ii. 4–6). The 'together' aspect is always the work of the Holy Ghost.

After the Resurrection we read that Our Lord breathed on the disciples and said, "Receive ye the Holy Ghost": i.e., He imparted to them the Holy Ghost who quickened them. On the Day of Pentecost we read that "there appeared unto them tongues distributing themselves, like as of fire"— and the disciples were baptized by the personal Holy Ghost:

25

the quickening became an equipment. "But ye shall receive power, after that the Holy Ghost is come upon you:" (Acts i. 8). The baptism of the Holy Ghost is the complete uniting of the quickened believer with Christ Himself.

"For by one Spirit are we all baptized into one body." The baptism with the Holy Ghost is not only a personal experience, it is an experience which makes individual Christians one in the Lord. The only way saints can meet together as one is through the baptism of the Holy Ghost, not through external organizations. The end of all divisions in work for God is when He changes fever into white-heated fervour. Oh, the foolish fever there is these days! Organizing this, organizing that; a fever of intense activity for God. What is wanted is the baptism with the Holy Ghost which will mean Our Lord's prayer in John xvii is answered— "that they all may be one; as Thou, Father, art in Me, and I in Thee, that they also may be one in us" (v. 21).

(III.) THE HABITATION OF THE HOLY GHOST IN THE MILITANT CHURCH.

". . . and gave Him to be the head over all things to the church, which is His body" (Ephesians i. 22).

The habitation of the Holy Ghost in the Church is not yet mature, it is easy to despise or ignore it. "The habitation of God through the Spirit" refers to the Christian community as it is in this dispensation, and it is an amazing mix-up! But Christ loves the Church so patiently that He will cleanse it from every blemish, and "present it to Himself a glorious church, not having spot, or wrinkle, or any such thing, . . ." (Ephesians v. 25-27).

The different offices of the Church are ordained of God and are based, not on the natural gifts of man, but on the spiritual gifts which Christ gave after He ascended ". . . and He gave some, apostles; and some, prophets; and some, evangelists; and some, pastors and teachers: for the *edifying* ("*building up*", R.V.) of the body of Christ" (Ephesians iv. 11-12); consequently the only sign that a particular gift

26

comes from the risen Christ is that it edifies the Church. Nothing else is of any account, no flights of imagination, no spiritual fancies, only one thing is of account, viz., the building up of men and women in the knowledge of the Lord. One essential difference between before Pentecost and after Pentecost is that from God's standpoint there are no great men after Pentecost. We make great men and women, God does not. No one is called now to be an isolated lonely prophet; the prophets are a figure of the whole Christian Church which is to be isolated collectively from the world.

There is a time coming when this earth will be the habitation of God, at present it is usurped by the world systems of men; when these disappear, then God's "new heaven and new earth" will emerge. (Revelation xxi. 1-3.)

THE GLORY OF THE LORD'S DISCIPLES

Acts i. 7–8

I. The Passing of Intellectual Christianity.

"It is not for you to know . . ."

Intellect is never first in spiritual life. We are not born again by thinking about it, we are born again by the power of God. Intellect comes second both in nature and in grace. The things we can express intellectually are the things that are old in our experience; the things that are recent and make us what we are, we cannot define. People say, 'You must believe certain things before you can be a Christian.' It is impossible. A man's beliefs are the effect of his being a Christian, not the cause of it. The evangelism which bases itself simply on justification by faith produces a hard type of mind, and when it becomes aggressive it produces the 'soul-saving' type. It is impossible to locate the 'soul-saving' idea in the New Testament. The glory of the Lord's disciples is not the saving of souls; but the 'soul of salvation' expressed in personal lives. It is God's work to save souls: "Go ye therefore and make disciples" (Matthew xxviii. 18–20). Have we been doing it? The New Testament emphasis is on living justly on the basis of salvation, i.e., expressing in our individual lives the things we believe.

II. The Power of Incarnate Christianity.

"But ye shall receive power, when the Holy Ghost is come upon you; and ye shall be My witnesses."

In the New Testament the emphasis is not on believing, but on receiving. The word "believe" means to commit —a commitment in order to receive. Have I ever received anything at all from God? The bedrock of Christianity is not decision for Christ, for a man who decides banks on his decision, not on God. It is the inability to decide— 'I have no power to get hold of God, no power to be what I know He wants me to be.' Then, says Jesus, "Blessed

28

are you." "Blessed are the poor in spirit: for theirs is the kingdom of heaven."

"and ye shall be My witnesses"—not witnesses of what Jesus can do or of His gospel, but witnesses unto Him, that is, He is perfectly satisfied with us wherever we are. The baptism of the Holy Ghost does not mean signs and wonders, but something remarkably other—a life transfigured by the indwelling of the Holy Spirit and the realization of the Redemption in personal experience. (See Acts iv. 13; Galatians iv. 19.) Historically, the baptism of the Holy Ghost added nothing to the apostles' doctrine, it made them the incarnation of what they preached. The great idea is not that we are at work for God, but that He is at work in us; not that we are devoted to a cause and doing aggressive work for God, but that He is working out a strong family likeness to His Son in us. "My witnesses" —the witness may or may not lead to martyrdom, but the indwelling of the Holy Ghost in us and the baptism of the Holy Ghost upon us, makes an expression of the life of Jesus that perfectly satisfies Him wherever we are.

III. THE PROGRAMME OF IDENTIFIED CHRISTIANITY.

"both in Jerusalem and in all Judea and Samaria, and unto the uttermost part of the earth."

God does the arranging of our programme. At certain stages of spiritual experience we feel we could do a lot if we could arrange the scene of our own martyrdom, but the Spirit of God reminds us that we do not choose the place of our offering (cf. Deuteronomy xii. 13–14). God has the setting of the saint's life. Everyone who is born from above wants to be a missionary, it is the very nature of the Spirit they receive, viz., the Spirit of Jesus, and the Spirit of Jesus is expressed in John iii. 16, "God so loved the world . . ." God keeps open house for the universe. "Lovest thou Me?" said Jesus, "Feed My lambs." We prefer to build up converts to our own point of view. Are we prepared to be the disciples of the Lord Jesus in whom the glory of God is manifested? Can God see the manifestation of His Son's life in us? "Everyone therefore that confesseth Me before men . . ." It is easy to be priggish and profess, but it takes the indwelling of the Holy Spirit to so identify us with Jesus Christ that when we are put in a corner we confess Him, not denounce others. 'No, I cannot take part in what you are doing because it would imperil my relationship to Jesus Christ.' We are afraid of being 'speckled birds' in the company we belong to. Jesus says, 'Don't be ashamed to confess Me.'

"But ye shall be baptized with the Holy Ghost . . ." (v. 5). Why do we want to be baptized with the Holy Ghost? All depends on that 'why.' If we want to be baptized with the Holy Ghost that we may be of use, it is all up; or because we want peace and joy and deliverance from sin, it is all up. "He shall baptize you with the Holy Ghost," not for anything for ourselves at all, but that we may be witnesses unto Him. God will never answer the prayer to be baptized with the Holy Ghost for any other reason than to make us witnesses to Jesus. To be consciously desirous of anything but that one thing is to be off the main track. The Holy Ghost is transparent honesty. When we pray, 'Oh Lord, baptize me with the Holy Ghost whatever it means,' God will give us a glimpse of our self-interest and self-seeking until we are willing for everything to go and there is nothing left but Himself. As long as there is self-interest and self-seeking, something has to go. God is amazingly patient. The perplexity is not because of the hardness of the way, but the unwilling pride of sin, the stubborn yielding bit by bit, when it might be done any second. The acceptance of the Divine nature involves in it obedience to the Divine precepts. The commands of God are enablings. God banks entirely on His own Spirit, and when we attempt, His ability is granted immediately. We have a great deal more power than we know, and as we do the overcoming we find He is there all the time until it becomes the habit of our life.

The baptism with the Holy Ghost is the great sovereign work of the personal Holy Ghost; entire sanctification is our personal experience of it.

30

THE BEST IS YET TO BE

John iv.

"The best is yet to be" is really true from Jesus Christ's standpoint. There is nothing noble the human mind has ever hoped for or dreamed of that will not be fulfilled, and a great deal more.

I. IN EMANCIPATING VISION.

"But this is that which was spoken by the prophet Joel; and it shall come to pass in the last days, saith God, I will pour out of My Spirit upon all flesh; and your sons and daughters shall prophesy, and your young men shall see visions, and your old men shall dream dreams: and on My servants and on My handmaidens I will pour out in those days of My Spirit; and they shall prophesy" (Acts ii. 16–18).

The vision of the agnostic, the socialist, the imperialist, or the Christian is the same; they all see the thing that is right—a time of peace on earth, a state of goodwill and liberty at present inconceivable. There is nothing wrong with the vision, and there is no difference in the vision, because its source is the Spirit of God. The thing to be criticized is not the vision, but the way in which the vision is to be realized. 'Your sons and daughters' refers to the men and women who have no concern about the redemptive point of view. The Spirit of God sways men who do not know Him, and they talk God's mind without a knowledge of Him personally. 'My servants and My handmaidens' are those who not only see the vision but have become personally related to Jesus Christ.

II. IN HAPHAZARD WAYS.

"And He must needs go through Samaria" (*v.* 4).

One great thing to notice is that God's order comes to us in the haphazard. We try to plan our ways and work things out for ourselves, but they go wrong because there are more facts than we know; whereas if we just go on with the days as they come, we find that God's order comes to us in that apparently haphazard way. The man who does not know God depends entirely on his own wits and forecasting. If instead of arranging our own programmes we will trust to the wisdom of God and concentrate all our efforts on the duty that lies nearest, we shall find that we meet God in that way and in no other. When we become 'amateur providences' and arrange times and meetings, we may cause certain things to happen, but we very rarely meet God in that way; we meet Him most effectively as we go on in the ordinary ways. Where you look for God, He does not appear; where you do not look for Him, there He is—a trick of the weather, a letter, and suddenly you are face to face with the best thing you ever met. This comes out all through the life of Jesus Christ; it was the most natural thing for Him to go through Samaria.

"And we know that to them that love God all things work together for good, even to them that are called according to His purpose" (Romans viii. 28). It is not faith to believe that God is making things work together for good unless we are up against things that are ostensibly working for bad. God's order does come in the haphazard, but only to those who love God; the only way in which God's order is recognized in our lives is by being what Jesus calls 'born from above'. God's order comes to us in the ordinary haphazard circumstances of life, and when we are in touch with Him the sacrament of His presence comes in the common elements of Nature and ordinary people. The real meaning of the word 'sacrament' is that the Presence of God comes through the common elements of the bread and the wine. If you are of a religious nature you will be inclined to put store on the symbol, but beware lest you put the symbol in the place of the thing symbolized; it is easy to do it, but once you mistake the symbol for what it symbolizes, you are off the track. "Consider the lilies of the field," said Jesus; we consider motor-cars and aeroplanes, things full of energy. Jesus never drew His illustrations from these things, but always from His Father's handiwork. A lily grows where it is put and does not fuss; we are always inclined to say 'I would be all right if only I were somewhere else.' If our spiritual life does not grow where we are, it will grow nowhere.

III. IN EXUBERANT VITALITY.

· "If thou knewest the gift of God, and who it is that saith to thee, Give me to drink; thou wouldest have asked of Him, and He would have given thee living water" (v. 10).

Jesus Christ never preached down to the level of His audience; He did not rely on human understanding, but on the interpreting power of the Holy Spirit in a human mind. The disciples frequently misunderstood what Our Lord said, but He banked everything on the work of the Holy Spirit. "Howbeit when He, the Spirit of truth, is come, He shall guide you into all the truth."

Jesus surprised the woman of Samaria by His extraordinary generosity of mind—"How is it that Thou, being a Jew, askest drink of me, which am a woman of Samaria? for the Jews have no dealings with the Samaritans." Our Lord knew who the woman was, but He did not talk with the smile of a superior person, 'My poor ignorant woman, when will you understand what I say?' He let her talk about what she knew, and she talked with a growing wonder behind it. The first thing Jesus did was to awaken in her a sense of need of more than she had, and until she got the length of asking—"Sir, give me this water," He did not say a word about her sin. We don't take Jesus Christ's way, our first aim is to convict people of sin; Jesus Christ's aim was to get at them where they lived. No man can stand the revelation of what he really is in God's sight unless he is handled by Jesus Christ first. Jesus Christ takes a *Saviour's* view of what is wrong, not a sentimental view. He gently and firmly handles what is wrong in order to remove it.

"If thou knewest the gift of God, . . . thou wouldest have asked of Him, and He would have given thee living water." Jesus is referring to the gift of the Holy Spirit. Unless I receive a totally new Spirit, all the believing and correct doctrine in the world will never alter me; it is not a question of believing, but of *receiving*. The symbol Jesus uses is that of a "well of water, springing up into everlasting life." 'Everlasting life' is the gift of God Himself; it springs up and expresses itself in a strong family likeness to Jesus. The great sign that a man has received the Holy Spirit is that he begins to manifest the fruits of the Spirit. Life manifests itself as *life*, not as nervous hysterics. "I am come that they might have life," said Jesus, "and that they might have it more abundantly." This 'well of water' is full of the ease and power of God which never exhausts itself, but continually recuperates us as we spend it out.

The message of the Gospel is not that God gives a man a clean heart, but that He gives him a pure heart. Jesus never says, 'Decide for Me,' but 'Come to Me in your absolute emptiness and let Me fill you.' Christianity is not a clean heart empty, which means a collapse sooner or later, but a life passionately full of personal devotion to Jesus Christ, and a determined identification with His interests in other men. "For the Father seeketh such to worship Him."

THE UNTENANTED UNIVERSE OF EASTER

"He appeared to me also" (1 Corinthians xv. 8).

Very few of us come to realize what is ours through the resurrected Lord, viz., that we can really draw on Him for body, soul and spirit now. We do not trust in a Christ who died and rose again twenty centuries ago; He must be a present Reality, an efficacious power now. One of the great words of God in our spiritual calendar is NOW. It is not that we gradually get to God, or gradually get away from Him; we are either there now or we are not. We may get into touch with God instanter if we will, not because of our merit, but simply on the ground of the Redemption; and if any man has got out of touch with God in the tiniest degree he can get back now, not presently; not by trying to recall things that will exonerate him for what he has done, but by an unconditional abandon to Jesus Christ, and he will realize the efficacious power of the resurrected Lord *now*.

To use the New Testament as a book of proof is nonsense. If you do not believe that Jesus Christ is the Son of God, the New Testament will not convince you that He is; if you do not believe in the Resurrection, the New Testament will not convince you of it. The New Testament is written for those who do not need convincing. After the Resurrection our Lord appeared to those only who knew Him in the days of His flesh. How many people recognized that the Carpenter of Nazareth was God Incarnate? Very few bothered their heads about Him; He was totally ignorable. The relationship to our Lord is a purely spiritual one, and the Resurrection brought out the personal relationship of each one—of Peter and John, Mary and Thomas (see John xx. and xxi.); and here the marvellously personal note is brought out—"He appeared to me also." Our Lord never sent out His disciples to proclaim the Gospel on the ground that He had done something for them, but only on the ground that they had seen Him. "But go unto My brethren, and say to them, . . ." Mary Magdalene was not sent on the ground that Jesus had cast seven demons out of her, but on the ground of the Resurrection. She knew now who Jesus was; before she only knew what He could do.

I. THE LAST WORD ABOUT MYSELF.

"and that He appeared to Cephas:" (1 Corinthians xv. 5).

Cephas was the man who but a little while before denied that he knew Jesus; he saw Him on the cross dead, and the last memory in his mind would be, 'Yes, and I did not stand by Him, I denied Him with oaths and curses.' Think of the agony of Peter's mind, and then think of this—'He appeared to Cephas.' Jesus came to His heart-broken disciple after His resurrection, no record is given of what took place; all we know is that Jesus reinstated Peter in public (see John xxi. 15–17). But read Peter's Epistles, they are full of the kindness of the Good Shepherd to the sheep.

The great essential bedrock of relationship to the resurrected Lord is that we know the last word about ourselves. Do I really know that I am a pauper spiritually? Then Jesus says, 'Blessed are you'. "Blessed are the poor in spirit: for theirs is the kingdom of heaven." The Easter message is that the Lord 'appeared to me also'. I know Him personally for myself.

Supposing I have been delivered from sin, would that necessarily assure me that I should know Jesus if I saw Him? Not the tiniest bit. Mary Magdalene had had seven demons cast out of her, but when she saw Jesus after the Resurrection she was blinded by grief and personal sorrow and she mistook Him for the gardener. I, too, may mistake Him for 'the gardener'. But the Eternal Resurrected Christ may touch me through the gardener. He may touch me through a child, through a flower. If I am in living personal relationship to Jesus the things that make the common affairs of life become conveyors of the real presence of God.

If you have come to the last word about yourself, watch for the Lord; He is there all the time, and He will come to you in some supernatural way. "Lo, I am with you all the days." It is not an effort of faith, but a marvellous realization.

II. THE LEAST WITNESS TO THE LORD.

"And last of all, as unto one born out of due time, He appeared to me also."

"To me also"—the most unlikely! It is easy to pretend to be 'less than the least' without being it, easy to be false in emotion before God, but Paul is not a pretentious humbug, he is not simply speaking out of the deep modesty of his soul, he is speaking what he believes. One of the greatest revelations is that Jesus does not appear to a man because he deserves it, but out of the generosity of His own heart on the ground of the man's need. Let me recognize I need Him, and He will appear. I believe many a man keeps away from Jesus Christ through a sense of honour—'I don't deny that God can forgive me, but I know what I am, and I don't want to let Him down.' Once let that man realize that Christianity is not a decision for Christ, but a complete surrender to let Him take the lordship, and Jesus will appear to him. He will do more, He will put into him a totally new heredity, the heredity that was in Himself. That is the amazement of regeneration. "If ye then, being evil, know how to give good gifts unto your children: how much more shall your heavenly Father give the Holy Spirit to them that ask Him?" (Luke xi. 13).

III. THE LIVING WAY BEFORE THE LORD.

"Thou art the Christ, the Son of the living God" (Matthew xvi. 16).

It is a marvellous thing to know that Jesus Christ is the Son of God, but a more marvellous thing to know that He is the Son of God in me. "But when it pleased God, who separated me from my mother's womb, and called me by His grace, to reveal His Son in me, that I might preach Him among the heathen; immediately I conferred not with flesh and blood:" (Galatians i. 15, 16). My relationship to Jesus is not on the ground of Christian evidences, that I can pass an examination on the doctrine of the Person of Christ, but suddenly by the great surprise of the indwelling Spirit of God I see who Jesus is, the Son of the Living God, absolute Lord and Master. The basis of the Christian life is an inner illumination that reveals to me who Jesus is, and on that revelation and the public confession of it, Jesus says He will build His church (Matthew xvi. 15-18).

The searching point is—Has Jesus appeared to me also? not simply am I saved and turned into another man, but do I know Him? is He evidencing His marvellous presence in me? Can I bank on Him not by an effort of faith, but by a real influx of His resurrection life? One of the greatest indications as to the way the Spirit of God deals with us is to notice where we are exhausted without recuperation. When by over-energy on our part, or over-calculation of our own, we undertake more than God has sanctioned, there is the warning note of weariness. If spiritual people would only take heed, they would find God's gentle warning always comes—'Not that way; that must be left alone, this must be given up; this is the course for you.'

The Living Way before the Lord is to keep in personal touch with Jesus Christ. Never take Jesus Christ as the Representative of God: He *is* God or there is none. If Jesus Christ is not God manifest in the flesh, we know nothing whatever about God; we are not only agnostic, but hopeless. But if Jesus Christ is what He says He is, then He is God to me.

Christianity is a personal history with Jesus. "and ye shall be My witnesses." The baptism of the Holy Ghost does not mean that we are put into some great and successful venture for God, but that we are a satisfaction to Jesus wherever we are placed. It is not a question of service done, but that our living relationship to Him is a witness that satisfies Him.

UNCENSORED TRUTH

"The twilight that I desired hath been turned into trembling unto me" (Isaiah xxi. 4).

The Bible never deals with the domains our human minds delight to deal with. The Bible deals with heaven and hell, good and bad, God and the devil, right and wrong, salvation and damnation; we like to deal with the things in between. The Bible pays no attention to our susceptibilities. "The twilight that I desired . . ." In the Bible there is no twilight, but intense light and intense darkness.

I. THE DESIRED NEUTRALITY.

"He that gathereth not with Me scattereth abroad" (Matthew xii. 30). Neutrality in religion is always cowardice —'I don't want to take sides'. God turns the cowardice of a desired neutrality into terror: "The twilight that I desired hath been turned into trembling unto me." Our Lord makes everything depend upon a man's relationship to Himself, not upon a man's goodness or badness. Twilight is a desirable time—not too strong a light and not too dark a dark; details are not too clearly manifested, ugly lines are not visible, everything looks wonderful. We like to get into the sentimental domain of twilight spiritually.

"Little children, let no man deceive you: he that doeth righteousness is righteous, even as He is righteous" (1 John iii. 7). The Apostle John won't allow 'twilight' in a child of God. There is no such thing as being neutral, we are either children of God or of the devil; we either love or we hate; the twilight is torn away ruthlessly. We are secretly unrighteous before God, not before men, we do not wish our secret sins dragged into the light of God's countenance; we object to the intense light of dawn, and desire twilight. When God's searching comes it is that kind of unrighteousness that is revealed, and we cannot say a word. We realize we have ignored God and have indulged in unrighteousness before Him.

II. THE SUDDEN CONVICTION OF NEMESIS.

"He that committeth sin is of the devil; for the devil sinneth from the beginning" (1 John iii. 8). Nemesis means retributive justice, something it is impossible to escape. We recoil when we realize the inevitable things in life, and it is the things we call inevitable that make us disbelieve in God. We are not conscious anarchists against God, we worship Him to a certain point, but immediately the Spirit of God begins to point out something in us that is wrong, we are offended (cf. John vi. 66, Matthew xi. 6).

As long as Jesus Christ will remain the 'meek and mild and gentle Jesus' I will listen to Him, but immediately He sets His face against my particular sin, my un-righteousness, my self-indulgence, I am going to have no more of Him; then the nemesis comes, and I realize that I am siding with the forces which are against Jesus Christ. Immediately God touches me or mine, I realize that I have the disposition of the devil in spite of all my religion and morality. There is a disposition in us that does not belong to human nature but to the devil, the spirit of unloving, unrighteous hatred. 'Develop your deepest instinct and you will find it to be God': Jesus says, "For from within, out of the heart of men, proceed . . ." If we live in the twilight we say, 'Those things are not in my heart.' The right attitude to the truth is, 'Lord, Thou knowest'; otherwise we shall find to our cost that what Jesus said about the human heart is true. We are all possible saints or possible devils. "Not as Cain, who was of that wicked one, and slew his brother" (1 John iii. 12). The spirit of Cain is jealousy, spite and envy. There is no hatred on earth like the hatred of a middling good man for the good man. The first civilization was founded by a murderer. There is something worse than war, and that is the average run of commercial business life in piping times of peace; it does not destroy a man's body, but it

40

almost damns his soul, it makes a man a cultured detester of the one who competes against him.

III. The Secret Condition of the Divine Nature.

"In this the children of God are manifest, and the children of the devil" (1 John iii. 10). Lovingkindness is the purest, rarest evidence of the indwelling of the Spirit of God—no more neutrality, no more dread of the nemesis, just the Divine nature, beautiful, pleasant beneficence, all summed up in the word 'Love'. When the love of God is shed abroad in our hearts it means that we identify ourselves with God's interest in other people, and God is interested in some strange people! Are we prepared to waive all our predilections and identify ourselves entirely with God's interests in other people? Is the Divine nature getting its way in us? Our actual conduct among men has to be moulded by the conduct of our Heavenly Father. When we think of the grudge we owe someone, let the Spirit of God bring back to our memory how we have treated God, and then begin to be His children. "He is kind toward the unthankful and evil" (Luke vi. 32–38). That is the actual practical climax of the teaching of the Sermon on the Mount. Never testify with your lips what your life does not back up.

THE LORD AS OUR 'DEAR DREAD'

"Then said Jesus, It is for judgment that I have come into this world, to make the sightless see, to make the seeing blind" (John ix. 39, Moffatt).

That is one of the stiff things Jesus said. It is either nonsense, or what we believe it to be—the very wisdom of God. There is no contradiction in that verse and John xii. 47—"For I came not to judge the world, but to save the world;" Jesus Christ did not come to pronounce judgment, He Himself is the judgment; whenever we come across Him we are judged instantly.

I. IN THE UNERRING DIRECTNESS OF HIS PRESENCE.

One of the most remarkable things about Jesus Christ is that although He was full of love and gentleness, yet in His presence every one not only felt benefited, but ashamed. It is His presence that judges us; we long to meet Him, and yet we dread to. We have all known people like that; to meet them is to feel judged, not by anything they say —we are rarely judged by what people say, but by their character.

(a) The Judgment of His Language.

People realized His judgment in His words, not in His pronouncements such as Matthew xxiii., but in His casual language, judgment came straight home. So with our friends, some casual word, a word not necessarily addressed to us at all, judges us and we feel our meanness, that we have missed the mark. Jesus did not stand as a prophet and utter judgments; wherever He went the unerring directness of His presence located men. We are judged too by children, we often feel ashamed in their presence; they are much more our judges than we theirs, their simplicity and attitude to things illustrates our Lord's judgments.

42

(b) *The Judgment of His Labours.*

The sense of judgment was brought home in the wonderful things Jesus did. When He told Peter to put out into the deep, and the multitude of fishes was so great that the boats began to sink, "Simon Peter fell down at Jesus' knees, saying, Depart from me; for I am a sinful man, O Lord." What Jesus did judged Peter absolutely. He did not say, 'You should have done what I told you without any demur,' He was simply ineffably and extraordinarily kind, and that drove the judgment home.

(c) *The Judgment of His Looks.*

It is not sentimental to say that the photograph of some people brings a sense of judgment; in certain moods we feel rebuked when we meet the look direct of someone we love, or look at their photo. If that is true of human beings, what must it have been of the looks of Jesus? "And the Lord turned, and looked upon Peter . . . And he went out and wept bitterly." I do not think there was any rebuke in His look—'How dare you do such a thing,' but a look of absolute God-likeness, and it brought the judgment home (cf. Mark x. 21; iii. 5).

It is not simply the things Jesus says to us directly, or what He does in the way of judgment particularly; it is Himself entirely, wherever He comes we are judged.

(d) *The Judgment of His Life.*

If you look at a sheep in the summer time you would say it was white, but see it against the background of startling virgin snow and it looks like a blot on the landscape. If we judge ourselves by one another we do not feel condemned (see 2 Corinthians x. 12); but immediately Jesus Christ is in the background—His life, His language, His looks, His labours, we feel judged instantly. "It is for judgment that I have come into the world." The judgment that Jesus Christ's presence brings makes us pronounce judgment on ourselves, we feel a sense of shame, or of missing the mark, and we determine never to do that thing

43

again. If Jesus Christ was only like a man, with a lynx eye for seeing everything that was wrong, we might be defiant. When someone with fiendish penetration unearths all we are, it does not bring judgment home to us, it awakens resentment and we glory in our badness; but when we come across the unerring directness of Jesus Christ's presence we feel as Peter felt—"Depart from me, O Lord." He felt unfit to be anywhere near Jesus.

II. In the Unexpected Discovery of his Presentations.

(a) *The Blindness of Human Judgment.*

Jesus said some astounding things. This is one of them— "I have come . . . to make the seeing blind." "For man looketh on the outward appearance . . ." As long as we deal with things theoretically, we think that the best thing to do. I see certain facts in your life, you see certain facts in mine, and we pass judgment on one another. Jesus says that our judgment is blind, it does not *see.*

(b) *The Blunders of His Judges.*

"Whom do men say that the Son of man is? And they said, Some say John the Baptist; some, Elijah; and others, Jeremiah, or one of the prophets" (Matthew xvi. 13–14). "He hath Beelzebub, and by the prince of the devils He casteth out devils" (Mark iii. 22). "Behold, a gluttonous man, and a wine-bibber, a friend of publicans and sinners!" (Matthew xi. 19). These are some of the blunders of the human judgments of Jesus.

(c) *The Astonishment of His Judgments.*

For instance, take Our Lord's judgment of Peter—"Thou art Simon the son of John: thou shalt be called Cephas (which is by interpretation Peter)." (That is, "Rock or Stone." R.V. marg.). (John i. 42). Any ordinary common-sense person would say it was absurd to call Peter a rock, he was the most impulsive, the most unreliable of all the disciples; and yet the judgment of Jesus proved to be

44

correct. Again, Jesus saw Nicodemus alone, and although he was a cowardly disciple, He spoke the most vital truth He ever spoke to him. Again, He talked to a sinful woman about worshipping God and about the gift of the Holy Spirit.

We are apt to think the judgments of Jesus are wrong, but when they come straight home in our personal lives we judge in the same way. At first we are certain that our common-sense is wise, that we see and understand; when Jesus comes He makes that seeing blind. The first coming of Jesus into a life brings confusion, not peace (see Matthew x. 34). When we receive the Holy Spirit the immediate manifestation is not peace and joy, but amazement, a sense of division instead of order, because we are being re-related to everything and seeing things differently: we had been seeing in a blind way. Before we received the Holy Spirit we used to have very clear and emphatic judgments, now in certain matters we have not even ordinary common-sense judgment, we seem altogether impoverished. The way Jesus judges makes us know we are blind. We decide what is the most sensible common-sense thing to do, then Jesus comes instantly with His judgment and confuses everything, and in the end He brings out something that proves to be the perfect wisdom of God. The judgments of Jesus are always unexpected; unexpected in every way, e.g., Matthew xxv. 37–40.

III. IN THE UNCEASING DELIBERATENESS OF HIS POWER.

"It is for judgment that I have come into this world."

Jesus says the Father ". . . hath given Him authority to execute judgment also, because He is the Son of man" (John v. 27). The first of His judgments and the last, are Himself—His presence, His words, His labours, His looks, His life; these judge us all through, and it is to be the same in the end. "Judge nothing before the time, until the Lord come." Our Lord is unceasingly deliberate, the beginning and the end of His judgment is the same; He will not pass a hasty judgment on us. When He comes He will judge us straightaway, and we shall accept His judgment.

There is no vindictiveness in Our Lord's judgments; He passes judgment always out of His personal love. To my mind the thought of the last Judgment is a superb comfort, because we know who is to be the Judge: Jesus is to be the Judge. He will not pass a judgment that scathes, we can give ourselves over to Him knowing perfectly well that there are certain things in us which must go, and we are only too willing for them to go, but they cannot go without our feeling the pain and the shame of ever having held to them.

When we have wronged someone we love, the hard thing is not that he says something against us, but that he does not. That is the way our Lord judges, by His kindness (cf. Luke xv. 21–4).

> No! I dare not raise
> One prayer, to look aloft, lest it should gaze
> On such forgiveness as would break my heart.

". . . not knowing that the goodness of God leadeth thee to repentance?" (Romans ii. 4).

Some passages in the New Testament are taken to refer to the Second Coming of Our Lord, but their real meaning is His presence (e.g., 1 Thessalonians ii. 19; iii. 13; v. 23; 1 John ii. 28). He may come at any minute into our minds, or into our circumstances, and suddenly we feel a sense of shame. He is a 'dear dread,' we long to see Him and yet we are afraid to, because we know His presence will bring judgment on the things that are wrong.

"For everyone that doeth ill hateth the light, and cometh not to the light, lest his works should be reproved" (John iii. 20). You instantly know when you are away from the light by the lust of vindication in yourself—'I know I am right,' and you may dispute it right up to the threshold of the Lord's coming, but when He comes, instead of vindicating yourself, you will feel like Peter, "Depart from me, O Lord."

"If any man have not the Spirit of Christ, he is none of His" (Romans viii. 9). When we have a ban of finality about our views, we do not exhibit the Spirit of Jesus, but the spirit of the Pharisee. We pronounce judgments, not

46

by our character or our goodness, but by the intolerant ban of finality in our views, which awakens resentment and has none of the Spirit of Jesus in it. Jesus never judged like that. It was His presence, His inherent holiness that judged. Whenever we see Him we are judged instantly. We have to practise the presence of Jesus and work on the basis of His disposition. When we have experienced the unfathomable forgiveness of God for all our wrong, we must exhibit that same forgiveness to others.

THE MIRACLE OF JOY

Joy is the great note all through the Bible. We have the notion of joy that arises from good spirits or good health, but the miracle of the joy of God has nothing to do with a man's life or his circumstances or the condition he is in. Jesus does not come to a man and say 'Cheer up,' He plants within a man the miracle of the joy of God's own nature. "Then will I go unto the altar of God, unto God my exceeding joy:" (Psalm xliii. 4). The stronghold of the Christian faith is *the joy of God*, not *my joy in God*. It is a great thing for a man to have faith in the joy of God, to know that nothing alters the fact of God's joy. God reigns and rules and rejoices, and His joy is our strength. The miracle of the Christian life is that God can give a man joy in the midst of external misery, a joy which gives him power to work until the misery is removed. Joy is different from happiness, because happiness depends on what happens. There are elements in our circumstances we cannot help, joy is independent of them all.

"That My joy might remain in you, and that your joy might be full" (John xv. 11).

What was the joy of Jesus? That He did the will of His Father, and He wants that joy to be ours. Have I got the joy of Jesus, not a pumped-up ecstasy? The joy of Jesus is a miracle, it is not the outcome of my doing things or of my being good, but of my receiving the very nature of God. In every phase of human experience apart from Jesus, there is something that hinders our getting full joy. We may have the fulfilment of our ambitions, we may have love and money, yet there is the sense of something unfulfilled, something not finished, not right. A man is only joyful when he fulfils the design of God's creation of him, and that is a joy that can never be quenched.

". . . who for the joy that was set before Him endured the cross, despising the shame" (Hebrews xii. 2).

What was the joy set before Jesus? The joy of bringing many *sons* to glory, not saved souls. It cost Jesus the Cross,

48

but He despised the shame of it because of the joy that was set before Him. He had the task of taking the worst piece of broken earthenware and making him into a son of God. If Jesus cannot do that, then He has not succeeded in what He came to do. The badness does not hinder Him, and the goodness does not assist Him.

"Ask, and ye shall receive, that your joy may be full" (John xvi. 24).

'Ask in My Name,' says Jesus, i.e., 'in My nature.' How can I have the nature of Jesus? By being born from above, by the Holy Spirit coming into me on the ground of the Redemption and putting into me the disposition of Jesus. It is all done by the miracle of God's grace. "For the Father Himself loveth you," it is the wonder of a complete communion between you and the Father.

There are crushing, unspeakable sorrows in this world. To any man with his eyes open, life is certainly not worth living apart from Jesus Christ. If it is worth living, it is because he is blind (see 2 Corinthians iv. 3–4). Am I going to live in a fool's paradise, or let God open my eyes?

The joy of God remained with Jesus, and He said, "I want My joy to be in you." The wonder of communion is that I know and believe that Jesus Christ has redeemed the world; my part is to get men to realize it and then devote themselves to Jesus. Am I willing to forgo every other interest and identify myself with Jesus Christ's interests in other people? ". . . that we may present every man perfect in Christ Jesus." The people who influence us are those who have stood unconsciously for the right thing, they are like the stars and the lilies, and the joy of God flows through them all the time.

"Thou wilt show me the path of life: in Thy presence is fulness of joy; at Thy right hand there are pleasures for evermore"—an eternity of gratitude. Am I grateful to God for showing me the way of life? "I am the Way," not creed, nor church, nor doctrine, but Jesus Christ. God can take any man and put the miracle of His joy into Him, and enable him to manifest it in the actual details of his life.

49

HIS VOICE

"and the sheep follow him: for they know his voice." (John x. 4.)

We do not use our ears to hear in the particular way our Lord means, we use them to listen to what our disposition wishes us to decipher, either from fear or desire, as the case may be. When we desire a thing we shut ourselves off from every other thing and concentrate on our desire, but the hearkening our Lord indicates springs from neither fear nor desire, but from an intense humility. When we are born again we are no longer muddled by idiosyncrasies, and we begin to listen irrespective of our disposition.

I. THE DISTRACTIONS OF INDIVIDUALITY.

"And they heard the voice of the Lord God . . .: and Adam and his wife hid themselves from the presence of the Lord God" (Genesis iii. 8).

In this verse the identification of voice with personality is clear. When individuality comes into conflict with God's voice, it desires not to hear it. Adam, in taking his right to himself, made individuality lord it over personality: communion with God was lost and he became tyrannical over himself and would allow no intimation from personality. Adam and Eve are not now saying of God's voice, 'Cause me to hear it'; they are hiding from His presence in fear. They have taken individuality, which is the God-created husk of personality, and made it god, and when the Creator, who speaks only in the language of personality, came, they were afraid. It is now self-realization, not God-realization. Self-realization is based on individuality which is entrenched in human nature through sin, and it effectually distracts us from wanting to hear God's voice. Anything that makes for the realization of individual relationships, individual well-being and development—that is the thing we want to

50

hear. When the voice of God comes it disregards all that, and it produces terror. We don't want God to cause us to hear His voice, we want God to establish and deify the voices that characterize our individuality, our notions of what we ought to be. Wherever there is self-realization, the voice of God is a continual embarrassment. Individuality ignores Jesus Christ; when He speaks our individual concerns make too much noise for us to hear His voice. "He that hath ears to hear, let him hear." Are we distracted from hearing God's voice by any form of individuality? If God says something not in accordance with my individual attitude to things, do I really want to hear His voice? Jesus Christ deals always with our personal relationship to Him; He totally disregards individuality; it does not come into His calculations and He has no consideration for it, because individuality is simply the husk, personality is the kernel.

II. The Delight of Intimacy.

"Thou that dwellest in the gardens, thy companions hearken for thy voice: cause me to hear it."

The companions of God, i.e., the angels and the saints, hear His voice. In God's garden God Himself is the cultivator and the producer, the refiner of its atmosphere and flowers, of its human and animal life, and everything.

The Detachment of Transfiguration—"And this voice we ourselves heard come out of heaven . . ." (2 Peter i. 19). When we are really detached from individuality, detached from every form of self-realization, we experience something which corresponds to Peter's experience on the Mount, and it is then that God says to us, "This is My beloved Son: hear ye Him." Not only do we hear God say, "This is My beloved Son: hear ye Him," but we have

The Devotion of Trustfulness—"And the sheep hear his voice: . . . and the sheep follow Him: for they know his voice" (John x. 3, 4). Trustfulness is based on confidence in God whose ways I do not understand; if I did, there would be no need for trust. There are many ways of "following the Lamb whithersoever He goeth" because we know His voice. His voice has no tone of self-realization in it, nor of sin, but only the tone of the Holy Ghost. His voice is essentially simple; it is "a still, small voice," totally unlike any other voice. The Lord is not in the wind, not in the earthquake or in the fire, but only in "a sound of gentle stillness."

If we have had a personal touch from Jesus it manifests itself in

The Desire of Inspiration—Our whole life is desirous of saying "Cause me to hear it." We discern not by faith, but by love, by intimacy with God. The Old Testament makes much of faith; the New Testament makes everything of the relationship of love; "Lovest thou Me? . . . Feed My sheep." ". . . the greatest of these is love." That is why our Lord placed Mary of Bethany's act so high; it was not an act of faith, but of absolute love. The breaking of the alabaster box revealed the unconscious sympathy of her spirit with Jesus Christ.

Have I this delight of intimacy, or am I trying to bend Almighty God to some end of my own? Am I asking Him to make me a particular type of saint? If through my love for Him I am discerning His voice, it is a proof that individuality has been effaced in the oneness of personal relationship. The real enemy to the delight of intimacy with Jesus is not sin, but individual relationships (cf. Luke xiv. 26). Distraction comes from intimacy with those who are not intimate with Jesus.

We can always know whether we are hearkening to God's voice by whether we have joy or not; if there is no joy, we are not hearkening. Hearkening to the voice of God will produce the joy that Jesus had. ". . . that My joy may be in you, and that your joy may be fulfilled." A life of intimacy with God is characterized by joy. You cannot counterfeit joy or peace. What is of value to God is what we *are*, not what we affect to be.

Is your life truly 'hid with Christ in God'? If it is, your continual request is—'Cause me to hear Thy voice.' Can we hear the voice in which there is no self-realization, no self-interest, no individual preference? Spiritual muddle comes because we have other interests and loyalties, and these loyalties break our intimacy with Jesus Christ. When there is the clash of self-realization, and individual preferences come in and compete, we have to put them on one side and remain loyal to our Lord and to nothing and no one else.

There is darkness which comes from excess of light as well as darkness which is caused by sin. There are times when it is dark with inarticulateness; there is no speech, no understanding, no guide, because you are in the centre of the light. Stedfastly endure the trial and you will get direction from it. "What I tell you in the darkness, that speak ye in the light." Darkness is the time to listen, not to speak; if you do speak, you will speak in the wrong mood; you will be inclined to criticize God's providential arrangements for other lives and to tell Him He has no business to allow these things. As long as you are in the dark you do not know what God is doing; immediately you get into the light, you discover it. "Because thou hast kept the word of My patience . . ." The test always comes along the line of patience.

THE DOCTRINE OF THE GREAT HOUR

"when it was yet dark, . . ." (John xx. 1).

There is twilight before night, and an infinitely deeper dark before dawn; but there are hours in spiritual experience darker than either of these, when the new day looks like disaster, and light and illumination have not yet come. There is no possible progress in personal life or national life without cataclysms, big crises, breaks. In our ordinary life we have the idea that things should gradually progress, but there comes a time when there is a tumble-up, a mixture of God and man and fiends, of crime and abomination, and all our idea of steady progress is done for, although there may be progress in individual lives. In the Bible there is the same idea. For instance, take what our Lord says about new birth—"Verily, verily, I say unto thee, Except a man be born again, he cannot see the kingdom of God" (John iii. 3). Some teachers make new birth a simple and natural thing, they say it is necessary, but a necessity along the line of natural development. When Jesus Christ talks about it He implies that the need to be born again is an indication of something radically wrong—"Marvel not that I said unto thee, Ye must be born again." It is a crisis. We like to talk about the light of God coming like the dawn, but it never does to begin with, it comes in a lightning flash, in terrific upheaval. Things do not go unless they are started, and the start of everything in history and in men's souls proves that the basis of things is not rational but tragic; consequently there must be a crisis.

I. THE DARK OF THE DARKEST DAWN.

"The first day of the week cometh Mary Magdalene early, when it was yet dark, . . ." (v. 1).

Can you imagine anything more completely dark than that? Mary Magdalene had had a wonderful history with

Jesus Christ, He had absolutely delivered her: "and certain women, which had been healed of evil spirits and infirmities, Mary called Magdalene, out of whom went seven devils, . . ." then she saw Him crucified before her eyes, and now she has come to mourn the biggest disaster of her life. "when it was yet dark"—no light or illumination.

Many may be going through this experience. The testimony they used to give, which was quite genuine, is not working now, they are in other conditions and it is no good; they work for all they are worth, but there is neither life nor power in it. The weakness of many a testimony is that it is based on what the Lord has done—'I have to testify to what God has done for me in order that other people may have the same thing done for them.' It sounds all right, but it is not the New Testament order of testimony. Jesus Christ never sent out a disciple on the ground that He had done something for him, but only because he had seen the Lord after He had done something for him (see John ix. 35–38). People testify to conversion and to the grace of God in their lives, but plainly they do not know Him. There is no question about His having emancipated them from sin and done a mighty work in them, but the great passion of the life is not Jesus Christ; their personal experience is not marked by Paul's words—"that I may know Him."

II. The Desolation of the Glorious Day.

"But Mary stood without at the sepulchre weeping" (v. 11).

Mary was standing weeping in absolute distress; it was the most desolating dawn she had ever known, and yet it was the dawn of the most glorious day she was ever to know. "And as she wept, she stooped down and looked into the sepulchre, . . ." It is a good thing to stoop as well as weep; there is more pride in human grief and misery than in joy and health; certain elements in human sorrow are as proud as the devil himself. There are people who indulge in the luxury of misery, they are always talking of the agonising and distressing things—'No one ever suffered as I do; there is a special element in my suffering, it is isolated.' At the back of it is terrific pride, it is weeping that will not stoop.

"and seeth two angels in white . . ." Mary was not at all surprised when through her tears she saw angels; there was only One whom she wanted and that was her Lord and Master. ". . . she turned herself back, and saw Jesus standing, and knew not that it was Jesus." Mary is standing face to face with Jesus Christ and yet she does not know Him; the obsession of her grief makes her mistake Him for the gardener. Mary had had a wonderful history with Jesus, but now in her desolation she does not know Him. We only see along the line of our prejudices until the surgery of events alters our outlook. We may have had an experience of what Jesus Christ can do and yet not have known Him. Suddenly at any turn He may come—'Now I see Him.' It takes all time and eternity to know God.

III. THE DIRECTION FROM THE GREAT DIVIDE.

"Jesus saith unto her, Mary" (v. 16).

In the midst of her grief, Jesus said one word which had in it all her personal history with Him—"Mary." If Mary had had no past history with Jesus Christ she would not have detected Him when He spoke that word. If you have had a past history with Jesus Christ, if He has delivered and emancipated you, when He speaks, He speaks with the volume of that intimacy of personal acquaintance and you know, not by hearing only, but implicitly all through you— 'It is the Lord! No one else could speak like that to me.'

"She turned herself, and saith unto him, Rabboni; which is to say, Master." Mary thought that Our Lord had come back to the old relationship—'He is back again!' But Jesus said, "Touch me not; for I am not yet ascended to My Father:"—'You can no longer hold Me under the evidence of your senses, no longer hold Me as a possession of your own individual life as before; the relationship now is one you cannot begin to conceive as yet—a relationship of identity with Me through the indwelling Spirit of God, and I am

56

going to the Father to make that possible.' ". . . but go to my brethren, and say unto them, I ascend unto My Father, and your Father; and to My God, and your God."

The direction from 'The Great Divide' is that it is connected instantly with the verb 'to Go,' never to stay and moon. As soon as we see Jesus and perceive who He is by His Spirit, He says 'Go'—'Go out into actual life and tell My brethren, not what I have done for you, but that I am risen.'

No one can tell another about Jesus until he has seen Him as He really is, the One who imparts His own life, i.e. Holy Spirit, an impartation from the Lord Himself.

Darkness is not synonymous with sin; if there is darkness spiritually it is much more likely to be the shade of God's hand than darkness on account of sin; it may be the threshold of a new revelation coming through a big break in personal experience. Before the dawn there is desolation; but wait, the dawn will merge into glorious day—". . . the light of dawn, that shineth more and more unto the perfect day." If you are experiencing the darkness of desolation on individual lines, go through with it, and you will find yourself face to face with Jesus Christ as never before. "I am come that they might have life,"—life in which there is no death—"and that they might have it more abundantly."

DESERT DAYS

"Beloved, think it not strange concerning the fiery trial which is to try you, as though some strange thing happened unto you: . . ." (1 Peter iv. 12).

We have no faith at all until it is proved, proved through conflict and in no other way. There are things in life equivalent to the desert. This war is a 'fiery trial,' it has come out against our faith in God's goodness and justice. Are we going to remain stedfast in our faith in God until we see all that contradicts our common sense transfigured into exactly what our faith believes it should be?

I. The Decree of the Desolating Desert.

"And unto Adam He said, Because thou hast hearkened unto the voice of thy wife, and hast eaten of the tree of which I commanded thee, saying, Thou shalt not eat of it: cursed is the ground for thy sake; in sorrow shalt thou eat of it all the days of thy life" (Genesis iii. 17).

In actual life there is a desolating desert, and it is there by the decree of God; the Bible knows nothing about what we call natural law. Back of the origin of the desert is the decree of God. The desolating desert is not a distress to God, it is completely within His grasp, although not within ours. The Moslems have a fine phrase for the desert—'The Garden of Allah.' One characteristic of the desert is its fierce, cruel, unshielding light. "The sun shall not smite thee by day . . ." Another characteristic of the desert is its storms; these are never beneficial, they are of the sirocco order, blighting, fierce and pitiless. Jeremiah describes them—"At that time shall it be said to this people and to Jerusalem, A dry wind of the high places in the wilderness toward the daughter of My people, not to fan, nor to cleanse" (ch. iv. 11). The sun as seen in the desert is not a benediction, the storms are not beneficial storms; and night in the desert is a desperate thing. It is all very well to think of the night in our own land, but night in the desert is appalling. Little bits of the desert are fascinating, but the real thing is terrible —"that great and terrible wilderness" (Deuteronomy i. 19).

The characteristics of the desert are the characteristics of God to a man when he tastes life as it is. Ibsen saw very clearly the desolating desert of life, i.e., the terrific penalty of sin, and he also saw God as He appears to a man awakened to the facts of existence. We are apt to say that Ibsen was pessimistic, but every man whose thinking has not been interfered with by his temperament is a pessimist. To think fair and square is not to see goodness and purity everywhere, but to see something that produces despair. When a man sees life as it really is there are only two alternatives—the Cross of Jesus Christ as something to accept, or suicide. We are shielded by a merciful density, by a curious temperament of hopefulness that keeps us blind to the desolating desert.

The reason the desert came is that man ate of the fruit of the tree of knowledge of good and evil. God placed the tree in the garden, but He did not intend that man should eat of its fruit; He intended man to know evil only by contrast with good, as Our Lord did. It is by the decree of God that the man who knows good by contrast with evil shall find life a desolating desert. When the cosmic order of earth and the moral nature of man are in touch with God, the order of the earth is beauty, and the order of human life is love. Immediately a man gets out of touch with God, he finds the basis of things is not beauty and love, but chaos and wrath.

The first Adam, the federal head of the race, swung the race on to the basis of wrath, and Jesus Christ, the Last Adam, swung the human race back on to the basis of love. The terms 'in Adam,' 'in Christ,' are not mystical terms, but actual revelations of man's condition. When we are 'in Adam' we get down to the desolating desert aspect of life. Take love—the most abiding thing about love is its tragedy; or life, the most desolating thing about life is its climax, death. When we are 'in Christ' the whole thing is reversed. We read that "Jesus advanced in wisdom and stature and in favour with God and men"—He never ate of the fruit of the tree of good and evil, He knew evil only by contrast with good. When a man is born from above the desolating desert aspect of life goes. There is no sadness now in natural love, it ends nowhere but in the heart of God; 'in Christ' life knows no death, it goes on more and more fully. If you want to know God's original design for man, you see it in Jesus Christ; He was easily Master of the life on the earth, in the air and in the sea, not as God, but as Man; it was the human in Jesus that was master.

II. The Devil and the Divine in the Desert.

"And immediately the Spirit driveth Him into the wilderness" (Mark i. 12).

In the Bible the devil is represented as the antagonist of Deity; Satan represents the self-interest of humanity. Our Lord's words "Get thee hence, Satan" (Matthew iv. 10; see also Matthew xvi. 23) refer to the interests of humanity in conflict with God's interests. In the temptation the devil antagonized the same thing that he antagonized in the first Adam, viz., oneness with God. Our Lord's unvarying answer was, "I came down from heaven, not to do Mine own will, but the will of Him that sent Me"—the very thing the first Adam refused to do. "Man shall not live by bread alone," said Jesus, "but by every word that proceedeth out of the mouth of God." As long as civilization prevents us noticing the desert and the basis of wrath, we do not need anything other than bread, and what bread means. The claim of Satan to our Lord was, 'You will get your Kingship of·men if You give them bread' (see John vi. 15). Jesus Christ's first obedience was to the will of His Father, and it is by the obedience of Jesus Christ as Son of Man that the whole human race is swung back again to God. It was there, in the desert, that Our Lord bound the strong man and overcame him. The strong man represents the whole of humanity vested in a personal presence enthroned as God. When the strong man rules, his 'goods,' i.e. the souls of men, are in peace; but when 'a stronger than he' comes, He upsets that rule, and "takes from him his whole armour wherein he trusted, and divideth his spoils" (Luke xi. 22).

Jesus Christ is the One who upsets the humanitarian reign. That is why in certain moods of individual as well as national experience, Jesus Christ is considered the enemy of mankind. "Think not that I am come to send peace on earth: I came not to send peace, but a sword" (Matthew x. 34).

III. THE DIRECTION IN THE DESERT. (Luke iii. 2; Galatians i. 11-17.)

The word of God came to John in the desert—"The word of God came unto John the son of Zacharias in the wilderness"; and to Paul—"But when it was the good pleasure of God . . . to reveal His Son in me . . . I went away into Arabia." The nutriment of a man's life comes when he is alone with God; he gets his direction in the desert experiences. The Psalmist says, "Before I was afflicted I went astray." King Hezekiah came face to face with death and the experience made just that kind of difference to him— "I shall go softly (as in a solemn procession) all my years in the bitterness of my soul" (Isaiah xxxviii. 15). Men learn in these ways that 'man doth not live by bread alone'; there are factors in life which produce terror and distress.

IV. THE DIVINE DEPARTURE OF THE DESERT.

"The wilderness and the solitary place shall be glad; and the desert shall rejoice, and blossom as the rose" (Isaiah xxxv. 1-2).

The Divine recovers the desert for man as a Garden. The sin of man has polluted the material earth and it will have to be disinfected (Isaiah xxiv. 1), and there will be "a new heaven and a new earth." The actual conditions of life will surpass all that Utopian dreamers have ever dreamed. "And death shall be no more; neither shall there be mourning, nor crying, nor pain, any more"—here-after, without the desert; no tears, no darkness, no sinful defect, no haunting thought, no sickness, no sorrow. *"It hath not entered into the heart of man to conceive the things which God hath prepared for them that love Him."*

IS HUMAN SACRIFICE REDEMPTIVE?

"Greater love hath no man than this, that a man lay down his life for his friends" (John xv. 13). *human*

"But God commendeth His own love toward us, in that, while we were yet sinners, Christ died for us" (Romans v. 8, R.V.). *Divine*

There is a vast difference between human sacrifice and Divine sacrifice. John xv. 13 refers to human sacrifice, the highest height to which a human being can get; Romans v. 8 refers to Divine sacrifice, that which God has done for the human race and which no man can ever do. "Greater love hath no man than this, that a man lay down his life for his friends." It has nothing to do with a man's religion; a pagan will lay down his life for his friend, so will an atheist, and so will a Christian; it has to do with the great stuff human nature is made of, there is nothing Divine about it. We find men who have been the greatest scamps in civil life doing the most heroic things in war.

The love of God is other than that—God laid down His life for His enemies, a thing no man can do. The fundamental revelation made in the New Testament is that God redeemed the human race when we were spitting in His face, as it were. We can all be stirred by high, noble, human sacrifice; it is much more thrilling than Calvary. Calvary is an ignoble thing, against all the ideas of human virtue and nobility; it is far more thrilling to talk about men fighting in the trenches. God's love is not in accordance with our human standards in any way.

In the generality of our thinking the Bible does not mean anything to us, other things are of more practical use, and we are apt to discard what the Bible says until we come up against things. The Bible speaks about the Redemption, viz., what God has done for the human race, not about what we can get at by our common sense. The great fundamental

63

revelation regarding the human race is that God has redeemed us. Redemption is finished and complete; but what does it mean in our personal lives? The fact of Redemption amounts to nothing in my actual life unless I get awakened to a sense of need. It is a matter of moonshine to me whether Jesus Christ lived or died until I come up against things—either sin in myself or something that ploughs deeply into me, then I find I have got beyond anything I know, and that is where the revelation of Jesus Christ comes in; if I will commit myself to Him, I am saved, saved into the perfect light and liberty of God on the ground of Redemption.

The Redemption is a revelation, not something we get at by thinking, and unless we grant that Redemption is the basis of human life we will come up against problems for which we can find no way out. I can no more redeem my own soul and put myself right with God than I can get myself upstairs by hanging on to my shoestrings—it is an impossibility; but right at the basis of human life is the Redemption. The Redemption means that God has done His 'bit': men are not *going to be* redeemed, they *are* redeemed. "It is finished," said Jesus on the Cross. But the way the Redemption works in my actual life depends on my willing attitude to the revelation. Every man is redeemed, and the Holy Spirit is here to rouse us up to the fact that we are redeemed. Once that realization dawns, the sense of gratitude springs up in a man and he becomes of use to God in practical life.

Human sacrifice can never be redemptive. How can a man, noble or ignoble, get me nearer God? He may stir and move me till I say, 'That is a magnificent deed,' but he tells me no more about God. Many a man without any knowledge of God has laid down his life in the same noble manner that a Christian has done. That is the greatest love of *man*. The love of *God* is that He laid down His life for His enemies in order that He might make the basis of life redemptive. We have to reason on that basis, viz., on what God has done for the human race. Think of the worst man or woman you know; can you say to yourself, with any degree of joyful certainty, 'That man, that woman—perfect in

Christ Jesus'? You will soon see how much you believe in Christ Jesus and how much in common sense.

The Gospel is not good news to men, but good news about God, viz., that God has accepted the responsibility for creating a race that sinned, and the Cross is the proof that He has done so. The basis of human life is the Redemption, and on that basis God can perform His miracles in any man, i.e., He can put a new disposition into me whereby I can live an entirely new life. Think of the relief that the Gospel brings to a man's mind, and then think of the abortion that is called the Gospel and is preached to men as good news!

The test of our religious faith is not that it does for us, but that it does for the worst blackguard we can think of. If the Redemption cannot get hold of the worst and vilest, then Jesus Christ is a fraud. But if this Book means anything it means that at the wall of the world stands God, and any man driven there by conviction of sin finds the arms of God outstretched to save him. God can forgive a man anything but despair that He can forgive him.

THE LIE IN THE GREATEST FEAR OF LIFE

"For He must reign, till He hath put all enemies under His feet. The last enemy that shall be destroyed is death" (1 Corinthians xv. 25–26).

The greatest fear in life is not personal fear for myself, but fear that after all God will be worsted. We do not state it in that way until we come to one of the rare, lucid moments in our experience. The phrase "He must reign" indicates our greatest fear, viz., the fear that in the end Jesus Christ will not come out triumphant, that evil and wrong will triumph. We reveal our fear by intense assertions that of course He will win through. That is the curious way we are built; we speak as intensely of a position about which we are fearful as we do of a position we are sure of. Whenever this particular fear assails us, we assert most definitely —'Oh, yes, there is no doubt that He will get through,' while our real fear is that He will not. We are familiar with it along other lines—in reading a book we turn to the end to see whether the hero gets through. Fears are facts; there is a danger of saying that because a thing is wrong, therefore it does not exist; fear is a genuine thing, there is no courage without fear. The courageous man is the one who overcomes his fear. There are things in personal experience and in national life that make us hold our breath; then in faith we look on to the end.

*fears are
facts !!*

I. THE FEARFUL HOUR.

"Then said Jesus unto the twelve, Will ye also go away?" (John vi. 66).

John describes the disappointment Jesus Christ was to men. The crowd on the outside gathered to Him because He did wonderful things and they would have made Him king (*v.* 15), but He disappointed them. "The Jews there-

66

fore murmured concerning Him, because He said, I am the bread which came down out of heaven" (v. 41). Then there was the smaller crowd on the inside who came because they were religious and had the intellect of the time, and they listened, until He said things that offended them— "Many therefore of His disciples, when they heard this, said, This is a hard saying; who can hear it?" (v. 60). Then there was the little crowd of disciples, and of these we read—"Upon this many of His disciples went back, and walked no more with Him" (v. 66); and Our Lord forecast the fearful hour of His being left by everybody—left by the crowd, by the Pharisees, and by the disciples, and He turns to the handful left and says, "Will ye also go away?" and Peter replies, in effect, 'We have gone too far.' The hearts of these disciples must have feared, not for their own sakes, but—'After all, are we mistaken in this Man? We have left our homes and our fishing, we have been thrilled by Him, He has done wonderful things, but will He win through after all?'

The question comes to us personally: "Will ye also go away?" and we say, 'I believe Jesus Christ will get through,' but at the same time the forces are so awful and so intense that we wonder. At the heart of the fear there is a lie, and the lie comes in because we estimate Jesus Christ in the way we would estimate any other man, viz., by success. It is significant that Jesus Christ told His disciples not to estimate themselves by success (see Luke x. 19–20). According to the ordinary standards of men Our Lord Himself is as a corn of wheat falling into the ground and becoming futile. "Except a corn of wheat fall into the ground and die, it abideth alone; but if it die, it bringeth forth much fruit" (John xii. 24). Look at the history of every vigorous movement born spontaneously of the Holy Ghost, there comes a time when its true spiritual power dies, and it dies in correspondence to the success of the organization. Every denomination or missionary enterprise departs from its true spiritual power when it becomes a successful organization, because the advocates of the denomination or of the missionary enterprise after a while have to see first of all to the establishment and success of their organization, while the thing which made them what they are has gone like a corn of wheat into the ground and died. One of the greatest snares of modern evangelism is this apotheosis of commercialism manifested in the soul-saving craze. I do not mean God does not save souls, but I do believe the watchword 'A passion for souls' is a snare. The watchword of the saint is 'A passion for Christ.' The estimate of success has come imperceptibly into Christian enterprise and we say we must go in for winning souls; but we cannot win souls if we cut ourselves off from the source, and the source is belief in Jesus Christ (John vii. 37). Immediately we look to the outflow, i.e., the results, we are in danger of becoming specialists of certain aspects of truth, of banking on certain things, either terror or emotionalism or sensational presentations—anything rather than remaining confident that "He must reign." If we stand true to Jesus Christ in the midst of the fearful hour we shall come to see that there is a lie at the heart of the fear which shook us. We are not called to be successful in accordance with ordinary standards, but in accordance with a corn of wheat falling into the ground and dying, becoming in that way what it never could be if it were to abide alone. After the corn is garnered into the granary it has to go through processes before it is ready for eating. It is the 'broken-bread' aspect which produces the faithfulness that God looks upon as success; not the fact of the harvest, but that the harvest is being turned into nutritious bread.

II. THE FORLORN HOPE.

"And when He rose up from prayer, and was come to His disciples, He found them sleeping for sorrow" (Luke xxii. 45).

The disciples had given up everything for Jesus; they had followed Him for three years; now He talks to them in a significant way about buying swords (v. 36), and Peter and the other disciples imagine that this is the time when He will break through and introduce His kingdom; and instead of watching and praying, they make up their minds where the struggle is to be. But what happened was the worst they had feared; instead of Jesus Christ showing any fight, He gives Himself up, and the whole thing ends in humiliating insignificance. Peter never dreamt he was going to see Jesus Christ give Himself up meekly to the power of the world, and he was broken-hearted and "followed Him afar off." To call Peter a coward for following Jesus afar off is an indication of how we talk without thinking Peter and all the disciples were broken-hearted, everything they had hoped for with regard to Jesus Christ had deliberately failed—'We trusted in Him and were perfectly certain He would win through,' and now their worst fears were realized, and "they all forsook Him and fled." Many a Christian since the day of Peter has suffered complete heartbreak, not because he fears anything personally, but because it looks as if his Lord is being worsted; the lie at the heart of the fear is almost succeeding.

The presentation of the spiritual aspect of things is that it is a forlorn hope always, and designedly so, in this order of things. We are apt to forget that we must go far enough back to find the basis on which things erect themselves. For instance, if civilized life is right and the best we can know, Christianity is a profound mistake; but if you turn back to the Bible you find that its diagnosis of civilization is not that it is the best we know, it is on an entirely wrong basis. Civilized life is based on the *reason* at the heart of things; Jesus Christ's teaching is based on the *tragedy* at the heart of things, and consequently the position of true spiritual life is that of the forlorn hope. It is of the nature of the earth on which we tread—"The meek shall inherit *the earth*," not the 'world,' because the world, according to the Bible, is the system of civilized things that men place on God's earth. In the meantime God's earth is like the earth we are on now; we can do what we like with it, shovel rubbish on it, mine it and turn it into trenches; we can score it, and make it the foundation for the erections of human pride; but Jesus Christ says, "the meek shall inherit *the earth.*" There is a time coming when the earth itself shall be the very garment of God, when the systems of the world and those that represent them shall call on the mountains and the rocks to hide them, but at that time the earth won't shelter them.

III. THE FAITH THAT TRIUMPHS.

"Jesus saith unto him, Thomas, because thou hast seen Me, thou hast believed: blessed are they that have not seen, and yet have believed" (John xx. 29).

Thomas was not an intellectual doubter, he was a temperamental doubter; there was not a more loyal disciple than Thomas, he was a loyal, gloomy-hearted man. He had seen Jesus killed; he saw them drive the nails through His hands and His feet, and he says, 'Except I shall see . . ., I will not, I dare not believe.' This is a man with a passionate desire to believe something over which he dare not allow himself to be deceived. Seeing is never believing: we interpret what we see in the light of what we believe. Faith is confidence in God before you see God emerging, therefore the nature of faith is that it must be tried. To say 'Oh, yes, I believe God will triumph' may be so much credence smeared over with religious phraseology; but when you are up against things it is quite another matter to say, 'I believe God will win through.' The trial of our faith gives us a good banking account in the heavenly places, and when the next trial comes our wealth there will tide us over. If we have confidence in God beyond the actual earthly horizons, we shall see the lie at the heart of the fear and our faith will win through in every detail.

70

DISCOVERY BY DEVOTION

"And I set my face unto the Lord God, to seek by prayer and supplications" (Daniel ix. 3).

I. THE DETERMINATION TO CONCENTRATE.

"And I set my face . . ."

We discern spiritual truth not by intellectual curiosity or research, but by entreating the favour of the Lord, that is, by prayer and by no other way, not even by obedience, because obedience is apt to have an idea of merit. If we are not concentrated we affect a great many attitudes; but when we 'set our faces unto the Lord God' all affectation is gone—the religious pose, the devout pose, the pious pose, all go instantly when we determine to concentrate; our attention is so concentrated that we have no time to wonder how we look. "This one thing I do . . ." says Paul; his whole attention was fixed on God. Is my mind fixed entirely on God or on service for God? If I am only fixed on the service of God my attention is not held, I am taken up with affectation; but in a great crisis, as in this of Daniel, there is the determination to concentrate. When I set my face and determine to concentrate I am not devoted to creeds or forms of belief or to any phase of truth, not to prayer or to holiness, or to the spreading of any propaganda, but unto God. We never turn to God unless we are desperate, we turn to common sense, to one another, to helps and means and assistances, but when we do turn to the Lord it is always in desperation (see Psalm cvii.). The desperation of consecration is reached when we realize our indolence and our reluctance in coming to God.

II. THE DESPERATION OF CONSECRATION.

". . . unto the Lord God,"

Belief is not that God can do the thing, but belief *in God*. If I believe in God I pray on the ground of Redemption and

71

things happen; it is not reasonable, it is Redemptive. Where reason says 'There is a mountain, it is impossible', I do not argue and say 'I believe God can remove it', I do not even see the mountain; I simply set my face unto the Lord God and make my prayer, and the mountain ceases to be (see Matthew xvii. 20). As long as we reason and argue and say 'It is not sensible', we do not turn to the Lord but try to bolster up some conviction of our own.

Through the desperation of consecration we not only reach the limit of reason but we get a line of recognition which is other than reasonable, i.e., we discern Jesus Christ in the most ordinary people and things. "Jesus stood on the shore: but the disciples knew not that it was Jesus." He appeared to be an ordinary fisherman, but John discerned that it was the Lord (John xxi. 4–7). When we are concentrated on God we enter on a life of revelation, we begin to penetrate and discover things. "To him that overcometh . . ." Life is given as we overcome—overcome the tendency to indolence, above all the tendency not to do what we know we should, and instantly we get a revelation.

III. The Discipline of Consciousness.

"to seek by prayer and supplications,"

It is easy to create a false emotion in prayer, nothing easier than to work ourselves up until we imagine we really concerned about a thing when we are not because it has never been brought to our mind by the Holy Spirit. That kind of prayer is not natural, we let our emotions carry us away. Prayer is not only to be about big things, but talking to God about everything—"Let your requests be made known". If we try to recall something by our own effort in praying, instantly we get an atmosphere of rebuke about another person. When we concentrate on God that spirit is not present, there is no irrelevant emotion to deflect our attention and we pray about the things the Spirit of God brings most naturally to our minds. "Ye shall ask whatsoever ye will . . ." We do not ask what our will is in, we develop false emotions, consciousnesses that are not really our own. A false emotion is one we have at rare times. What is ours is the circumstances we are in just now, the people we are with; we have to learn to school our emotions into relationship to God in all these things. The seeking by prayer is determined by the circumstances we are in and by the life we habitually live; we have to concentrate on the ordinary obvious things we are in all the time. We cannot talk to God unless we walk with Him when we are not talking. The Son of God revealed in me and the epistle of Christ written in my life day by day will give me an expression before God; if I am not walking with God I have to borrow other people's phrases when I pray. "If any man is in Christ there is a new creation", everything becomes amazingly simple, not easy, but simple with the simplicity of God.

LOSING OURSELVES

"He that findeth his life (soul) shall lose it and he that loseth his life (soul) for My sake shall find it" (Matthew x. 39—R.V. marg.).

"We *are* what we are interested in."

'Soul' refers to the way a personal spirit reasons and thinks in a human body. We talk about a man exhibiting 'soul' in singing or in painting, that is, he is expressing his personal spirit. 'If you are going to be My disciple,' says Jesus, 'you must lose your soul, i.e., your way of reasoning, and acquire another way.' When the Holy Spirit energizes my spirit, my way of reasoning begins to alter, and Jesus says unless I am prepared for that, I cannot be His disciple. It takes a long time to acquire a new way of reasoning, the majority of us who are inclined to be earnest Christian people simply deal with the fact of spiritual experience without any spiritual reasoning. We have to acquire the new soul with patience (Luke xxi. 19).

I. THE UNDISCOVERED TERRITORY OF CONSCIOUS REALIZ-
    ATION.

"He that findeth his life . . ."

There is nothing more highly esteemed among men than self-realization, but Jesus says that "that which is highly esteemed among men is abomination in the sight of God". We are apt to have the notion that all Jesus Christ came to do was to deliver morally corrupt people from their corruption. A man is largely responsible for the corruption of his actual life; Jesus Christ does not deal with my morality or immorality, but with 'my right to myself'. Whenever our Lord talked about discipleship He always said 'IF'— '*If* any man will be My disciple, let him deny himself', not deny himself things as an athlete does, but 'let him give up his right to himself to Me'. If I am going to know Jesus

Christ as Lord and Master I must realize what I have to forgo, viz., the best thing I know, my right to myself. It is easy to say, 'Yes, I am delighted to be saved from hell and put right for heaven, but I don't intend to give up my right to myself'. Apart from Jesus Christ, conscious self-realization is the great thing—the desire to develop myself. My natural self may be noble, but it is a moral earthquake to realize that if I pursue the conscious realization of myself it must end in losing my ideal of life. It is a tremendous revelation when I realize that self-realization is the very spirit of antichrist. Self-realization is possible in the spiritual domain as well as the natural; much of the 'Higher Spiritual Life' teaching is simply self-realization veneered over with Christian terms. For a man to be set on his own salvation, on his own whiteness, to want to be 'the one taken', is not Christian. The great characteristic of our Lord's life is not self-realization, but the realization of God's purposes.

Self-realization may keep a man full of rectitude, but it is rectitude built on a basis that ultimately spells ruin, because man is not a promise of what he is going to be, but a magnificent ruin of what human nature once was. If we go on the line of conscious self-realization, there will be an aftermath of bitterness.

II. THE UNTRACEABLE TROUBLES OF CONSECRATED RENUN-
    CIATION.

". . . shall lose it; and he that loseth his life . . ."

In certain stages of spiritual life God is dealing with us on the death side and we get the morbid conception that everything we have, we must give up—'the everlasting "No" '. In the Bible the meaning of sacrifice is the deliberate giving of the best I have to God that He may make it His and mine for ever: if I cling to it I lose it, and so does God. We come to our renunciations in the same way that Abraham came to his. God told Abraham to offer up Isaac for a burnt offering, and Abraham interpreted it to mean that he was to kill his son; but on Mount Moriah Abraham lost a wrong tradition about God and got a right insight as to what a burnt offering meant, viz., a *living* sacrifice (Romans xii. 1–2). It looks as if we had to give up everything, lose all we have, and instead of Christianity bringing joy and simplicity, it makes us miserable; until suddenly we realize what God's aim is, viz., that we have to take part in our own moral development, and we do this through the sacrifice of the natural to the spiritual by obedience, not denying the natural, but sacrificing it.

Christianity is a personal relationship to Jesus Christ made efficacious by the indwelling Holy Spirit. We take Christianity to be adherence to principles. Conscience is not peculiarly a Christian thing, it is a natural asset, it is the faculty in a man that fits on to the highest he knows. Our convictions and conscientious relationships have continually to be enlarged, and that is where the discipline of spiritual life comes in. A man who is on the grousing line has no brightness or joy, no time for other people, he is taken up with the diseases of his own mind.

III. THE UNHINDERED TRIUMPHS OF CHRIST-REALIZATION.

". . . for My sake shall find it."

The characteristic of Christianity is abandon, not consciously setting myself on my own whiteness; the one thing that matters is, is Jesus Christ getting His way? The Christianity of the New Testament is not individual, it is personal, we are merged into God without losing our identity—"that they may be one, even as We are one". Individuality is the husk of the personal life, it cannot merge; personality always merges.

Am I prepared to lose my soul, lose the miserable self-introspection as to whether I am of any use? I am never of any use so long as I try to be. If I am rightly related to Jesus Christ, He says, 'Out of you will flow rivers of living water'. The people who tell are those who don't know they are telling, not the priggish people who worship work.

76

Am I prepared to go through death to my right to myself, to have 'a white funeral' and abandon myself to Jesus Christ—"for My sake"? If I am, I shall 'find my soul'. The Holy Spirit coming into my personal spirit manifests itself in my soul, in the way I reason, consequently all my previous calculations are upset and I begin to see things differently. In the initial stages of discipleship you get 'stormy weather', then you lose the nightmare of your own separate individuality and become part of the Personality of Christ, and the thought of yourself never bothers you any more because you are taken up with your relationship to God.

THE IMMENSE ATTENTION OF GOD

"And when he opened the seventh seal, there followed a silence in heaven about the space of half an hour" (Revelation viii. 1).

If we are ever going to understand the Book of the Revelation we have to remember that it gives the programme of God, not the guess of a man. "Write the things which thou hast seen, and the things which are, and the things which shall be hereafter." The Apostle is writing what the Spirit revealed to him—that is the origin of the Book. Apocalyptic literature is never easy to understand, its language is either a revelation or fantastic nonsense. We study it and worry over it and never begin to make head or tail of it, while obedience will put us on the line of understanding. Spiritual truth is never discerned by intellect, only by moral obedience. God brings His marvels to pass in lives by means of prayer, and the prayers of the saints are part of God's programme.

The presentation of Christianity which is not based on the New Testament produces an abortion—that a man's main aim is to get saved and put right for heaven; New Testament Christianity produces a strong family likeness to Jesus Christ and a man's notions are not centred on himself. The great aim of the Holy Spirit is to get us abandoned to God.

God allows the prayers of the saints, those who have entered into an understanding of His mind and purpose, to be brought to Him. We are busy praying that our particular phase of things may succeed, that men's souls may be saved; but what is meant by 'a saved soul' is frequently determined by our doctrine of salvation and not by a personal relationship to Jesus Christ. We are devotees of one tiny phase of what Jesus Christ came to do: He came not only to save men's souls, but to bring 'many sons to glory'. We have lost out on that line altogether, we who are the saved souls

78

—where has been the production of disciples? That is not our line, it has no success, it cannot be tabulated. There has been no silence in heaven over our prayers, they have not entered into the programme of God, they have not been based on the Redemption; we have had no concern for the revelation of Jesus Christ, only for a particular phase of our own.

The whole idea of the prayers of the saints is that God's holiness, God's purpose, and God's wise ways may be brought about irrespective of who comes or goes. The notion has grown almost imperceptibly that God is simply a blessing machine for men—'If I link myself on to God He will see me through'; instead, the human race is meant to be the servant of God, a different thing altogether. If some of us are ever going to see God we shall have to go one step outside our particular relationship to things, religious or otherwise, and step into the revelation that Jesus Christ is our Lord and Master as well as our Saviour.

God is using us in His own purposes, we have to remain true to His honour. "Though He slay me, yet will I wait for Him" (Job xiii. 15)—that is the true nobility of the saint. Are we praying on the authority of the Redemption or on the ground of a preconceived notion of our own? Do we really believe that the basis of human life is Redemption? If we do, we shall no longer look for logical results, we shall look for God to work His own results, and His results work within certain moral frontiers (e.g., John v. 44). If we are outside those frontiers, we cannot see God; inside the frontiers we see Him at once. The prayers of the saints either enable or disable God in the performance of His wonders. The majority of us in praying for the will of God to be done say, 'In God's good time', meaning 'in my bad time'; consequently there is no silence in heaven produced by our prayers, no results, no performance.

Have our prayers demanded the immense attention of God? Have they been linked on to the basis of Redemption, or are we praying, for instance, on the line that God must bless the Allies in this war because they are in the right?

79

The result of the war will not be simply a national result. Men have not enlisted 'For King and Country', but for a deeper reason, and in the final issue our prayer should be that the British Empire may be God's servant as well as His instrument.

Are we adding to the prayers of the saints or becoming sulky with God if He does not give us what we want, so taken up with the 'nobility of man' that we forget what our calling is as saints? As saints we are called to go through the heroism of what we believe, not of stating what we believe, but of standing by it when the facts are dead against God. It is easy to say 'God is love' when all is going well, but face a woman who has gone through bereavement and see if you find it easy to say it. There is suffering which staggers your mind as you watch it, and yet those who go through it are sustained in a way we do not understand. Every day lives are passing by us, how much of the silence of heaven have we broken up by our prayers for them? How much of our praying is from the empty spaces round our own hearts and how much from the basis of the Redemption, so that we give no thought for ourselves or for others, but only for Jesus Christ?

Inarticulate prayer, the impulsive prayer that looks so futile, is the great thing God heeds more than anything else because it is along the line of His programme. A prayer offered by the humblest and most obscure saint on the ground of the Redemption of Jesus Christ demands the complete attention of God and the performance of His programme.

HIS FACE IN THE RIDDLE OF THE UNIVERSE

"But we see Jesus, . . . crowned with glory and honour" (Hebrews ii. 9).

Supposing there was a certain region of earth about which you knew nothing and you received a communication from someone who said 'I have never been to the country but this map is a sure guide'; and you also received a communication from someone who sent you no map but who said, 'I have been to this country myself and if you will trust yourself to me I will guide you straight there'; how absurd it would be to trust to the information which was not first-hand and not go with the one who had been there and knew the way. In all the problems of life there are any number of 'maps', all more or less guesswork, but Jesus says, '*I am the Way*.' There are people who tell us they have 'maps' of what is beyond this seclusion of earth, but Jesus Christ is the only One who has not only been on this earth, but beyond it, consequently He alone is our guide. Have we confidence in Jesus, or have we only a 'map'? The 'maps' lead astray, Jesus Christ is the only One who knows; any number of things may confuse us, but nothing confuses Him.

I. UN-MADE OR MADE BY THE GRAVE SECLUSION. (2 Corinthians v. 1–4.)

We are shut up to this physical world; other planets may be inhabited, we are shut up to this one—shut up to our five senses and to this earth. Some minds are un-made when they realize this seclusion, other minds are made because they see God's purpose in it. "We that are in this bodily frame do groan," says Paul, "earnestly desiring to be clothed upon with our house which is from heaven . . ." 'I would rather be away from this body,' he says, 'but yet to abide in the flesh is more needful for your sake, so I remain with joy because it is God's will.' When people get fanatical it is the barriers they go against, the barriers placed by birth and death, the barriers of sex. If we try to get out of the body by spiritualistic means or by suicide we shall have no guide; but if we get out of it in the providence of God and by faith in Jesus, there is no darkness or desperation—"O death, where is thy sting? . . . Death is swallowed up in victory." When people are puzzled by the grave seclusion they are in and try to push away the barriers, they get out into the open before they are ready and are likely to become unhinged in mind; but if 'we see Jesus', there is no perplexity. Regarding the hereafter, He has said, "Let not your heart be troubled, . . . I go to prepare a place for you." Can we see Jesus in everything concerning ourselves, or are we trying to defy the barriers, wasting our time wishing we were somewhere else? The only way not to evade the problems of our grave seclusion in the body is by seeing Jesus and being devoted to Him.

The way we see the world outside us depends entirely upon our nervous system, and the marvel of God's construction of us is that we see things outside us as we do. For instance, the existence to us of beauty and colour and sound is due entirely to our nervous system: there is no colour to me when my eyes are shut, no sound when I am deaf, no sensation when I am asleep. If you want to know the most marvellous thing in the whole of creation, it is not the heavens, the moon and the stars, but—"What is man that Thou art mindful of him? Thou madest him to have dominion over the works of Thy hands." The whole of creation was designed for man, and God intended man to be master of the life upon the earth, in the air and in the sea; the reason he is not master is because of sin, but he will yet be. (See Romans viii. 19–22.) Paul indicates that the problems of the grave seclusion we are in are accounted for by sin, yet it remains true that our nervous system is not a disease, but is designed by God to be the temple of the Holy Ghost. The greatest proof of this is that Jesus Christ became the inhabiter of a nervous system like our own; He took upon Him the likeness of man and dwelt upon the earth. "If any man is in Christ Jesus, he is a new creature", that is, he has a totally new way of looking at things because he has a new disposition and begins to see things differently. Take two men in the desert, in the same regiment—one is in love, the other has committed sin; to the one the desert blossoms as the rose, to the other there is no beauty in anything. The difference is not in external setting, but in the ruling disposition. One day we shall be changed, "in a moment, in the twinkling of an eye", and the things which we see by means of our nervous system will suddenly take on another guise.

II. UN-DAUNTED OR DAUNTED BY THE GREAT SCHEME· (2 Peter iii. 8–13.)

The great scheme is the scheme of civilized life upon this earth. The apostle says, "Seeing that these things are all to be dissolved, . . ." he does not say 'destroyed', but 'dissolved'. What men have built upon the earth without any regard for God will be destroyed. The great scheme is that the physical universe which we see will be transfigured, i.e., become translucent with light. When our Lord was transfigured we read that "His garments became glistering", transfigured by indwelling light, and Peter indicates that the earth will go through its transfiguration and only what is holy will be able to live upon it. Now, we are limited to our body; then, we shall be transfigured in it. The way Jesus manifested Himself after the Resurrection is an indication of what we will be like when everything is related to God, we shall do things which seem miracles to us now. Jesus Christ was master of the elements because of His relation to God as Man, and in Him we see God's original design for man.

"Nevertheless we, according to His promise, look for new heavens and a new earth, wherein dwelleth righteousness." The Apostles were not daunted by the great scheme of things because they were looking for something else, the coming of the Day of God. If you think of the great scheme apart from seeing Jesus, you will be daunted by it. When civilized life goes into the crucible, as it is doing just now, men lose their wits, Jesus said they would; but to His disciples He said, "When ye hear of wars and rumours of wars: *see that ye be not troubled.*" The revolution is proving that the revelation given by Jesus Christ is true. Men are finding the 'maps' which they have taken as their guide are useless, they do not touch the basis of things, and as long as men refuse to take the direction of Jesus Christ wars and upheavals cannot be prevented; if they will take Him as their Guide they will find that things are slowly and definitely working toward the great scheme of "new heavens and a new earth, wherein dwelleth righteousness." Never look at actual things as if they were all; look at actual things in the light of the real, i.e., in the light of Jesus Christ.

III. Un-demented or Demented by the Grand Society.
(Revelation iii. 20; John xiv. 23.)

The way we get demented, off our balance, is by dreaming of what is yet to be—the Utopian vision of the grand state of society when all men are going to be brothers. It is not the vision that is wrong, it is right, what is wrong is the way men are trying to bring it about, and if they don't look to Jesus Christ they easily get unbalanced. Think what the Bible says is going to be! "Death shall be no more, neither shall there be any mourning, nor crying, nor pain, any more; . . . no more anything accursed; . . . but God Himself shall be with them, and He shall wipe away every tear from their eyes." Meantime there are tears, and sorrow and sighing, but though "we see not yet all things put under him, *we see Jesus*, crowned with glory and honour." Tears are not going to be wiped away by our receiving pettings from God; the revelation is that through the marvel of the Redemption God is going to make it impossible for there to be any more crying or sorrow, all will be as satisfactory as God Himself.

The writers of the New Testament look forward to the

grand society, but they do not become unbalanced because they are based on the Redemption. The aim of the grand society is not to be good, but to become the associates of God—"We will come unto him, and make our abode with him"; and the crown is—"they shall walk with Me in white; for they are worthy." We are to see God's face and confer with Him: "and His servants shall do Him service; and they shall see His face."

CLIMATE AND SPIRITUAL LIFE

"And He awoke and rebuked the wind, and said unto the sea, Peace, be still. And the wind ceased and there was a great calm." (Mark iv. 39).

This verse is a picture of our own spiritual life; there are occasions, such as this war, when it looks as if God were asleep, as if all our prayers were of no use; there are breakers ahead and it looks like destruction. But when He awakes in us, He calms the storm and rebukes our unbelief.

The life of Our Lord exhibits the influence of character on climate. It is easy to make this absurd, but looked at from the attitude of the Spirit of God you find there is an amazing connection between the storm and distresses and wild confusion of the earth just now and the waywardness and wrong of man; when the waywardness of man ceases and the sons of God are manifested, then "the creature itself also shall be delivered from the bondage of corruption into the glorious liberty of the children of God."

The Bible reveals that there is a close connection between character and climate. Ruskin is almost the only writer who recognizes it, and in this respect he is akin to the great prophets. The reason for the connection is fundamental. According to the Bible revelation, God created man a mixture of dust and Deity, and when the Redemption comes to its full scope, the whole earth is going to partake in it. Because man's body and his earthly setting have been affected by sin, we are apt to think that being made of the dust of the ground is his shame; the Bible implies that it is his chief glory, because it is in that body that the Son of God was manifested.

I. THE WAY OF GOD AND THE DAWN.

"And in the morning, a great while before day, He rose up and went out, and departed into a desert place, and there prayed." (Mark i. 35).

Specific times and places and communion with God go together. It is by no haphazard chance that in every age men have risen early to pray. The first thing that marks decline in spiritual life is our relationship to the early morning. It is significant that before nations have been gripped by civilization they always began their day early. (An American on visiting England after a lapse of years made this significant remark—'One thing that strikes me is the difference in the time people get up; twenty years ago everybody used to be astir early, but now I notice they rise much later.') When we are in touch with the earnestness of things, we begin soon.

(a) *The Devotion of Our Lord*. "And it came to pass in those days, that He went out into a mountain to pray, and continued all night in prayer to God. And when it was day, He called unto Him His disciples"; (Luke vi. 12–13).

It is not a haphazard thing, but in the constitution of God, that there are certain times of the day when it not only seems easier, but it *is* easier, to meet God. If you have ever prayed in the dawn you will ask yourself why you were so foolish as not to do it always: it is difficult to get into communion with God in the midst of the hurly-burly of the day. George MacDonald said that if he did not open wide the door of his mind to God in the early morning he worked on the finite all the rest of the day— "stand on the finite, act upon the wrong." It is not sentiment but an implicit reality that the conditions of dawn and communion with God go together. When the day of God appears there will be no night, always dawn and day. There is nothing of the nature of strain in God's Day, it is all free and beautiful and fine. "And there shall be night no more."

(b) *The Difference of Administration*. "Now late on the sabbath day, as it began to dawn toward the first day of the week, came Mary Magdalene . . ." (Matthew xxviii. 1).

Mary Magdalene thought that this dawn would be like an ordinary one, but it was the dawn of the greatest day, not only for Mary Magdalene but for the whole world. Our

Lord told her that there would be a different administration —'Till now you have known Me as God manifest in the flesh, now it is to be a knowledge after the Spirit; I will be in you, an indwelling Presence.' Penetration into truth comes when we choose the times God has chosen for us. All through the Old Testament the 'first' is dedicated to God; whenever that was neglected the prophets rebuked the people (e.g., Malachi iii. 8–9). We all know when we are at our best intellectually, and if instead of giving that time to God we give it to our own development, we not only rob God, but rob ourselves of the possibility of His life thriving in us. We heard it said that we shall suffer if we do not pray; I question it. What will suffer if we do not pray is the life of God in us; but when we do pray and devote the dawns to God His nature in us develops, there is less self-realization and more Christ-realization.

(c) *The Direction of Our Lord.* "But when day was now breaking, Jesus stood on the beach . . . And He said unto them, Cast the net on the right side of the boat, and ye shall find." (John xxi. 4, 6).

We have special times and days when we expect God to do things, but He usually does them when we don't expect it, e.g., when we are coming back in the early morning from fishing, it is then that God gives us direction. It is not simply that it is easier to get direction in the early morning, it is a profound revelation that that is the time when direction comes.

II. THE WILDERNESS OF TEMPTATION—THE DEVIL AND THE DIVINE.

"And Jesus, full of the Holy Spirit, returned from the Jordan, and was led by the Spirit in the wilderness during forty days, being tempted of the devil." (Luke iv. 1–2).

When artists or poets of earlier days wanted to depict a particular type of man they painted or described in words the climatic and geographical setting agreeing with that type. For instance, if they wanted to portray a man in

an angry temper, they put in the scenery of a thunderstorm.
Dante does it in the 'Inferno' and Milton in 'Paradise Lost'.
The outward is the symbol of the inner, according to the
Bible: there is a closer connection between them than we
imagine. When our supreme temptation comes, the setting
we are in, whether it is a city or the actual desert, brings us
into contact with the foundation of things as God made
them. According to Genesis, the basis of physical material
life is chaos, and the basis of personal moral life, wrath. If
I live in harmony with God, chaos becomes cosmos to me,
and the wrath of God becomes the love of God. If I get out
of touch with God I get into hell, physically and morally;
when I live in relationship to God by the inner witness of
the Spirit, "Heaven above is brighter blue, earth around a
sweeter green . . ."

(a) *The Desertion of a Disciple.* "And Satan entered into
Judas who was called Iscariot, being of the number of the
twelve." (Luke xxii. 3).

There was the wilderness of temptation in the lives of the
disciples; in one disciple the devil conquered absolutely and
Judas became what Jesus called him, "the son of perdition."
The popular idea of temptation is that it is towards evil,
meaning that we can see it to be evil by our common sense,
but temptation is always a short cut to good, the mind is
perplexed—'I wonder if this is the way of God?' If I yield
to the temptation the devil gets his way, as he did with Judas
in the last extreme.

(b) *The Desperation of a Disciple.* "And the Lord turned,
and looked upon Peter . . . And he went out and wept
bitterly." (Luke xxii. 61-2).

The devil tried to get Peter where he got Judas, but he
did not succeed; Satan did not 'enter into' Peter; Peter got
the length of denying Jesus, but in his wilderness of temptation he 'struck' the Divine, Judas 'struck' the devil; consequently Peter experienced a desperation producing tears,
and those tears were the most amazing bitterness in his life.
Peter with his impulsive heart would feel he could never
forgive himself, he would have spent the rest of his days

mourning, but Jesus had told him beforehand, "And do thou, when once thou hast turned again, establish thy brethren."

(c) *The Defeat of the Devil.* "Then the devil leaveth Him." (Matthew iv. 11).

Jesus Christ met the devil in the wilderness and defeated him. When you go through a time of trial, a wilderness of temptation in heart or mind or spirit, you feel inclined to get away out into somewhere like the desert. The reason for that is not haphazard, but because in the primal constitution of God man is connected with the dust of the earth: he is related to the elemental condition of things all through. When the sons of God are manifested the desolate place will alter at once. 'The desert shall rejoice, and blossom as the rose.'

III. THE WALL OF GOD AND THE DARKNESS ON THE DEEP.

"And it was now dark and Jesus had not yet come to them. And the sea was rising by reason of a great wind that blew." (John vi. 17–18).

This happens in our own lives—we are on the deep, it is dark, and Jesus is not there. It is a description of every elemental experience, such as bereavement or heartbreak, or any of the big things that beset human life, there is real speechless terror and misgiving. You may have had communion with God in the dawn, you may have continued with Jesus in temptation, but this thing makes you feel helpless—there is no way out. In times of deep sorrow it is not the people who tell you why you are suffering who are of any use; the people who help you are those who give expression to your state of mind, often they do not speak at all, they are like Nature. Nature is never heartless to the one who is bereaved, but it takes a revelation to make us know this.

(a) *At the Request of Jesus.* "And He said unto them, Let us go over unto the other side of the lake; and they launched forth." (Luke viii. 22).

'If you obey Jesus you will have a life of joy and delight.'
Well, it is not true. Jesus said to the disciples—"Let us go
to the other side of the lake," and they were plunged into
the biggest storm they had ever known. You say, 'If I had
not obeyed Jesus I should not have got into this complica-
tion.' Exactly. The problems in our walk with God are
to be accounted for along this line, and the temptation is
to say, 'God could never have told me to go there, if He had*
done so this would not have happened. We discover then
whether we are going to trust God's integrity or listen to
our own expressed scepticism. Scepticism of the tongue is
only transitional; real scepticism is wrung out from the man
who knows he did not get where he is on his own account
—'I was not seeking my own, I came deliberately because
I believe Jesus told me to, and now there is the darkness
and the deep and the desolation.'

(b)` *The Revelation of Jesus.* "But Simon Peter, when he
saw it, fell down at Jesus's knees, saying, Depart from me;
for I am a sinful man, O Lord." (Luke v. 8).

The revelation of Jesus comes in the way He walks on
our deeps; He tells us to do something which in the light of
our own discernment sounds ridiculous, but immediately we
do it, we experience the judgment of Jesus. The judgment
is not in what He says, it is Himself. "Depart from me,
O Lord," said Peter, but that was the last thing Peter wanted
Him to do, it was the impulsive expression of his state of
mind.

(c) *At the Rebuke of Jesus.* "And He arose, and rebuked
the wind, and said unto the sea, Peace, be still. And He
said unto them, Why are ye so fearful? how is it that ye
have no faith?" (Mark iv. 39–40).

Our Lord rebuked the disciples for fearing when apparently they had good reason for being alarmed. The problem
is—if Jesus Christ is only the Carpenter of Nazareth, then
the disciples were foolish to put Him at the tiller; but if
He is the Son of God, what are they alarmed about? If
Jesus Christ is God, where is my trust in Him? If He is
not God, why am I so foolish as to pretend to worship Him?

"And they feared exceedingly, and said one to another, What manner of man is this, that even the wind and the sea obey Him?" (v. 41).

Just where Jesus does not seem to be, when it looks as if the waves would overwhelm them, the Son of God comes walking on the top of those very billows. As we go on in our spiritual life we get into similar conditions, they are not •symbolic, but the actual conditions of our lives. God engineers us out of our sequestered places and brings us into elemental conditions, and we get a taste of what the world is like because of the disobedience of man. We realize then that our hold on God has been a civilized hold, we have not really believed in Him at all. When we get out on to the deep and the darkness we realize what a wonderful thing the Psalmist says—"Therefore will we not fear, though the earth be removed . . ." But it takes some confidence in God to say that when everything you trust in has gone.

IV. THE WORD OF GOD AND ELEMENTAL DESTRUCTION.

"Therefore whosoever heareth these sayings of mine, and doeth them, I will like him unto a wise man, which built his house upon a rock: and the rain descended, and the floods came, and the winds blew, and beat upon that house; and it fell not: for it was founded upon a rock, . . ." (Matthew vii. 24-27).

Our Lord reveals that the elemental destructions cannot touch us, neither death nor hell, nor all the forces of man and the devil put together, can prevail against the word of God if once we build on that; but if we build on our own discernment, then when the elemental destructions come, not only do we go, but our foundations go too. Our foundations must be rooted in God, then when the upheavals come we do not need to be afraid.

(a) *The Cosmic Power of Discernment.* "And then shall they see the Son of man coming in the clouds with great power and glory." (Mark xiii. 24-27).

The cosmic powers belong to God, and the great changes that will take place when He establishes His Kingdom will

92

reveal that the Son of Man and the cosmic powers are identified. "The meek shall inherit the earth," not the world; the world is not God's; the world is the name given to the system of things men have placed on God's earth, and the Bible foretells the time when these shall pass away; they are going into the crucible just now. Poets talk about Nature being 'the garment of God', and it will be true literally. We look for God in little ways, and He is there in all the terrific powers of Nature. We shall discern Him "in the clouds," i.e., the great elemental powers, when 'the heavens shall pass away . . . and the elements shall melt with fervent heat, and there will be new heavens and a new earth, wherein dwelleth righteousness.'

(b) *The Conscious Person and Divinity.* "And He was transfigured before them. And His raiment became shining, exceeding white as snow." (Mark ix. 2–3).

Our Lord emptied Himself of His glory when He became Incarnate, and here on the Mount the glory which He had with the Father before the world was suddenly burst through; the material part of Him was shot through with glory, that is, God and matter became one. That is what would have happened to the human race if Adam had not sinned, there would have been no death, but transfiguration. The counterpart of the Transfiguration is not the Resurrection, but the Ascension.

(c) *The Comprehensive Presence and Direction.* "Go ye therefore, and make disciples of all the nations, . . . and lo, I am with you alway " (Matthew xxviii. 19–20).

Jesus Christ teaches us to build our confidence in the abiding reality of Himself in the midst of everything. If a man puts his confidence in the things which must go, imagine his incomprehensible perplexity when they do go. No wonder Jesus said 'men's hearts failing them for fear.' These words describe the time we are in now. Our true life is not in the things which are passing, and if we build ourselves on God and His word, when they go, the marvel is that we are not scared. The thing to examine spiritually is, am I connected with Jesus Christ personally? If I have

93

only a form of belief or a creed, all that may go when the elemental trouble comes and I shall have nothing to cling to, but if I build my 'house' on the words of Jesus and do them, then no matter what happens I shall find I am founded upon the Rock.

THE NAME

"And His name shall be called Wonderful, . . ." (Isaiah ix. 6).

In the New Testament 'name' frequently stands for 'nature'. When we pray 'in the Name of Jesus' the answers are in accordance with His nature, and if we think our prayers are unanswered it is because we are not interpreting the answer along this line.

I. THE EXPRESSION OF GOD'S THOUGHT.

"And the Word became flesh, and dwelt among us, . . ." (John i. 14).

It is easy to get vague when we think about the thought of God; the poet talks about hearing God's voice on the rolling air, or as coming to us in the love of our friends; it sounds beautiful, but it may be all nonsense. Our sense of the beautiful has to take shape somehow, an ideal is of no use to me unless it has become incarnated. Nowhere in the Bible is there any notice taken of the worship of abstractions. We may talk about God as the Almighty, the All-powerful, but He means nothing to us unless He has become incarnated and touched human life where we touch it; and the revelation of Redemption is that God's Thought did express itself in Jesus Christ, that God became manifest on the plane on which we live.

(a) The Time-Beginning of God's Thought. (Genesis i. 2.)

When the mind of God thought on the chaos it was like an artist mixing the colours on his palette, and Genesis i. 2 describes the state of the 'palette'—"without form and void"; and out of that God created Cosmos; He expressed His thought in the universe we see. The earth is always spoken of in the Bible as God's. The word of God produces its own expression. "And God said, Let there be light: and there was light". Our language rarely expresses us at all.

(b) *The Time-Birth of God's Thought.* (John i. 1–3.)

God's Thought expressed itself not only in the universe which He created, but in a Being called "the Word", whose name to us is 'Jesus Christ'. John declares that God's Thought manifested itself in a Word, and that that Word became incarnated in a human life. We only know God's thought and the expression of it in Jesus Christ, and we only know the meaning of 'God and man one' in Jesus Christ. Our conception of the Trinity is an attempt of the human mind to define how God manifested Himself.

(c) *The Timeless Benediction of God's Thought.* (Philippians ii. 9–11, Ephesians i. 21.)

Jesus Christ not only has dominion now, but in the ages to come. God never says to man 'You must'; He says, 'You will ultimately come there.' We may come in the right way or by breaking our neck, but we will come, not by compulsion but by absolute agreement that Jesus Christ alone is The Way. God has so decreed it that man must work together with Him and bring about agreement with His own expressed Thought. We are apt to make the mistake of thinking that God is going to coerce men; He never does. God is giving men ample time to do exactly what they like, both as individuals and as nations; He allows us to develop as we choose, but in the end we will come to agree with Him. The introduction of socialism into the history of civilization is the next thing to be manifested, everything else has been tried, and socialism will end as every other human attempt has ended, in proving that man cannot establish himself in unity with God and ignore Jesus Christ, either in individual or in national life.

II. THE EDUCATION IN GOD'S THOUGHT.

"Ye are our epistle" (2 Corinthians iii. 2).

You cannot prove that God is love if you have not been born from above, because everything around you disproves it. Take the war and the ruination going on just now, it is absurd to say that it is just and reasonable; it is tragic and wrong; and yet when you are born from above you are able to 'discern the arm of the Lord' behind it all, but it takes the nature of Jesus Christ to see it, human nature apart from Him is unable to do so. "Marvel not that I say unto thee, Ye must be born again" Jesus said to Nicodemus. I must have the nature of Jesus Christ born into me, then I shall see things as He did.

(a) *The Character of the Name.* (Matthew i. 21.)

". . . and thou shalt call His name JESUS: for it is He that shall save His people from their sins." The character of the Name is that Jesus Christ is Saviour, and the evidence that I belong to Him is that I am delivered from sin; if I am not, I have a name to live, but am dead. When I become a Christian Jesus Christ exhibits the character of His own Name in me.

(b) *The Curriculum of the Name.* (Acts iv. 12.)

This verse is a profound utterance, the inevitable certainty that there is no salvation under heaven, saving through the Name of Jesus. The whole of our education is to bring us to this understanding. So often we are like a man crossing a moor who obstinately refuses to take any directions, and he goes on and on only to find himself hopelessly lost; then he humbly tracks back to the signpost and looking up, sees the way to go. God does not get angry with us, He simply waits until we realize that what He says is true. "And in none other is there salvation: for neither is there any other name under heaven, that is given among men, wherein we must be saved."

(c) *The Comprehension of the Name.* (1 Corinthians xii. 3.)

We blunder when we tell people they must believe certain things about Jesus Christ; a man cannot believe until he knows Him, then belief is spontaneous and natural. "No man can say, Jesus is Lord, but in the Holy Spirit." You may get a parrot recital of a creed, but when a man says, with a thrill all through him, 'Thou art the Christ', he is stating an intuitive revelation, not an intellectual conception; it is a committal to a Person. When I commit myself to Jesus I begin to see properly. No man believes what he sees unless he believes before he sees. "Because thou hast seen Me, hast thou believed? Blessed are they who have not seen, and yet have believed."

III. THE EXPERIENCE AS GOD'S THOUGHT.

We become incorporated into God's Thought, and then we go on to experience it. It will take all Time and Eternity to experience God's Thought—"And this is life eternal, that they should know Thee . . ."—a continual new wonder. The schooling we are going through just now is to develop us into an understanding of the Thought of God.

(a) *The Charge of the Name.* (Matthew x. 32.)

The charge of the Name means that I stand true to Jesus Christ, confessing Him wherever I am. It is easy to preach, nothing easier, but it is another thing to confess. Confessing means to say with every bit of me that Jesus Christ has come into my flesh. In practical outcome it means that if I say I have been saved by God's grace, I must show it, I have to be true to the Name in every detail. "By their fruits ye shall know them."

(b) *The Charm of the Name.* (Revelation ii. 17.)

Think of the way God disciplines us into an experience of the phases of the Name; sometimes we are chastened into knowing Jesus Christ as the Way, at other times into knowing Him as the Truth, and the Life; but there is another and a grander Name yet—"a new name, which no one knoweth but he that receiveth it."

(c) *The Community of the Name.* (Ephesians iv. 13.)

We attain to the fulness of Christ in one way only, through the Name. It is not individuals who attain, but humanity as a whole. One day the whole human race will be in God's sight as the Body of Christ, completely one with God. Jesus Christ was the Word of God, the expression of God's thought, and His earthly life is a symbol of what the human race will be like when it is related to God as the Son of Man was related. ". . . till we all come in the unity of the faith, and of the knowledge of the Son of God, unto a perfect man, unto the measure of the stature of the fulness of Christ."

HAVE I TO FORGIVE MY ENEMIES?

Matthew v. 43–48

Did Jesus Christ mean it when He said "Love your enemies"? If He did, we must come to the conclusion either that He was a madman, or that there is a meaning underneath His words which we do not at first see. It is impossible to do what Our Lord says if we imagine we can do it of ourselves, and we soon discover our ignorance. Jesus Christ bases all His teaching on the fundamental fact that God can do for a man what he cannot do for himself. It is an easy business to say I love my enemies when I haven't any, but when I have an enemy, when a man has done me or those who belong to me, a desperate wrong, what is my attitude as a Christian to be? Does Jesus Christ mean that I have to ignore the rugged sense of justice which is in every man, and be a sentimentalist and say, 'Oh yes, I forgive you'? What we are up against just now is the danger of not making the basis of forgiveness and peace the right kind. If it is not the basis of perfect justice, it will fail. We may succeed in calling a truce, but that is not peace, and before long we will be at it again.

I. THE MATTER OF FORGIVENESS. REPENTANCE. (Ephesians i. 7.)

"In whom we have redemption through His blood, the forgiveness of sins, according to the riches of His grace."

Forgiveness is the great message of the Gospel, and it satisfies a man's sense of justice completely. The fundamental factor of Christianity is "the forgiveness of sins." But what about the man who does not care whether he is forgiven or not? That is the case with us all to begin with, we do not care whether Jesus Christ lived or died or did anything at all, and to hear about God forgiving us, why, there is nothing in it. But when a man gets convicted of

100

sin (which is the most direct way of knowing that at the basis of life there is a problem too big for him to solve), he knows that God dare not forgive him; if He did, then man has a bigger sense of justice than God. The majority of us know nothing about the Redemption or forgiveness until we are enmeshed by the personal problem—something happens which stabs us wide awake and we get our indifferent hide pierced; we come up against things and our conscience begins to be roused. When once a man's conscience is roused he knows God dare not forgive him and it awakens a sense of hopelessness. Forgiveness is a revelation—hope for the hopeless; that is the message of the Gospel.

According to the Bible the basis of things is tragic, and the way out is the way Jesus Christ made in the Redemption. Any man, whether he be Cain or Judas, or you or I, can receive absolute forgiveness from God the moment he knows he needs it: but God cannot forgive a man unless he repents. Repentance means that we recognize the need for forgiveness —'hands up, I know it.' Jesus Christ did not come to fling forgiveness broadcast; He did not come to the Pharisees, who withstood Him, and said He was possessed with a devil, and say 'I forgive you': He said, "How can you escape the damnation of hell?" We may talk as much as we like about forgiveness, but it will never make any difference to us unless we realize that we need it. God can never forgive the man who does not want to be forgiven. As long as we live in the 'tenth storey' we either talk sentimental stuff or else we remain indifferent to the fact of forgiveness; only when we 'strike bottom' morally do we begin to realize what the New Testament means by forgiveness. Immediately a man turns to God, the Redemption is such that forgiveness is complete.

"In whom we have redemption through His blood, the forgiveness of sins." The background of the forgiveness of God is His holiness. If God were not holy, there would be nothing in His forgiveness. The conscience of God means that He has to completely forgive and finally redeem the whole human race. Every man knows by the way he is

101

made that there is such a thing as justice, and God forgives on the basis of *His* justice, viz., on the ground of Redemption. We are apt to say glibly that God will forgive us, but when we come up against the thing we know He dare not; if He did, He would cease to be God. There is no such thing as God overlooking sin. That is where people make a great mistake with regard to God's love; they say 'God is love and of course He will forgive sin': God is *holy* love and of course He *cannot* forgive sin. Therefore if God does forgive, there must be a reason that justifies Him in doing it. Unless there is a possibility of forgiveness establishing an order of holiness and rectitude in a man, it would bɛ a mean and abominable thing to be forgiven. If I am forgiven without being altered by the forgiveness, forgiveness is a damage to me and a sign of unmitigated weakness on the part of God. A man has to clear God's character in forgiving him. The revelation of forgiveness in the Bible is not that God puts snow over a rubbish heap, but that He turns a man into the standard of Himself, the Forgiver. If I receive forgiveness and yet go on being bad, I prove that God is not justified in forgiving me. When God forgives a man He gives him the heredity of His own Son, and there is no man on earth but can be presented 'perfect in Christ Jesus.' Then on the ground of the Redemption, it is up to me to live as a son of God. The reason my sins are forgiven so easily is because the Redemption cost God so much.

II. THE METHOD OF FORGIVENESS. REACTION. (Matthew vi. 12–15.)

Jesus Christ taught His disciples to pray "Forgive us our debts, as we forgive our debtors," that is, He taught them to recognize that God's method of forgiveness is the same as our own. Jesus Christ did not say '*because* we forgive our debtors,' but "*as* we forgive our debtors," that is, as children of God we are forgiven not on the ground of Redemption, but on the ground that we show the same forgiveness to our fellows that God has shown to us. 'For if ye forgive men their trespasses, your heavenly Father will also forgive you: but if ye forgive not men their trespasses, neither will your Father forgive your trespasses." God's method in forgiveness is exactly the method of our forgiveness, and is according to our human sense of justice.

Peter seemed to stand on tiptoe once and try to reach to God's forgiveness—"Lord, how oft shall my brother sin against me, and I forgive him? till seven times? Jesus saith unto him, I say not unto thee, Until seven times; but Until seventy times seven." Yet when a man has deliberately done you a wrong, it is according to the teaching of Jesus that you must not say you forgive him unless he turns; if he turns, forgiveness is to be complete. We may forgive easily because we are shallow, but when we are deeply roused, we cannot forgive unless our sense of justice is satisfied. The most marvellous ingredient in the forgiveness of God is that He also forgets, the one thing a human being can never do. Forgetting with God is a divine attribute; God's forgiveness forgets. We can never forget saving by the sovereign grace of God. God exhausts metaphors to show what His forgiveness means—"I, even I, am He that blotteth out thy transgressions for Mine own sake, and will not remember thy sins" (Isaiah xliii. 25); "I have blotted out, as a thick cloud, thy transgressions, and, as a cloud, thy sins" (Isaiah xliv. 22); "As far as the east is from the west, so far hath He removed our transgressions from us" (Psalms ciii. 12); "For Thou hast cast all my sins behind Thy back" (Isaiah xxxviii. 17); "For I will forgive their iniquity, and I will remember their sin no more" (Jeremiah xxxi. 34).

When the prodigal son came back with words which meant, 'I am sorry to the backbone for what I have done and am ashamed of myself,' the father never said a word about the far country, about the harlots and the riotous living (the elder brother reminded him of all that); he did not cast up at him one thing he had done—sufficient for him that his son had returned. Is it conceivable to us
103

that God will forget what we have done? He says He will; but the forgiveness of God does not work unless we turn; it cannot, any more than it does according to human justice. When we turn to God and say we are sorry, Jesus Christ has pledged His word that we will be forgiven, but the forgiveness is not operative unless we turn, because our turning is the proof that we know we need forgiveness.

III. THE MESSAGE OF FORGIVENESS. RETALIATION *v.* RETRIBUTION. (Matthew xviii. 15–17; 34–35.)

"Moreover if thy brother shall trespass against thee, go and tell him his fault between thee and him alone: if he shall hear thee, thou hast gained thy brother" (*v.* 15).

It would be an immoral thing to forgive a man who did not say he was sorry. If a man sins against you and you go to him and point out that he has done wrong—if he hears you, then you can forgive him; but if he is obstinate you can do nothing; you cannot say 'I forgive you,' you must bring him to a sense of justice. Jesus Christ said, "I say unto you, Love your enemies," but He also said the most appallingly stern things that were ever uttered, e.g., ". . . *neither will your Father forgive your trespasses.*" I cannot forgive my enemies and remain just unless they cease to be my enemies and give proof of their sorrow, which must be expressed in repentance. I have to remain stedfastly true to God's justice. There are times when it would be easier to say 'Oh well, it does not matter, I forgive you,' but Jesus insists that the uttermost farthing must be paid. The love of God is based on justice and holiness, and I must forgive on the same basis.

There is a difference between retaliation and retribution. The basis of life is retribution—"For with what judgement ye judge, ye shall be judged, and with what measure ye mete, it shall be measured to you again." This statement of our Lord's is not a haphazard guess, it is an eternal law and it works from God's throne right down. Life serves back in the coin you pay. You are paid back what you give, not necessarily by the same person; and this holds with regard to good as well as evil. If you have been generous, you will meet generosity again through someone else; if you have been shrewd in finding out the defects of others, that is the way people will judge you. Jesus Christ never allows retaliation, but He says that the basis of life is retribution. If my enemy turns and gives proof of his sorrow, I am not to meet him with retaliation. Christianity is not a set of principles, but relationship to a Person, Jesus Christ, while the Holy Spirit works in us a spontaneous relationship to things on the basis of God's forgiveness of us.

The distinctive thing about Christianity is forgiveness, not sanctification or my holiness, but forgiveness—the greatest miracle God ever performs through the Redemption. Forgiveness means not merely that a man is saved from sin and made right for heaven—no man would accept forgiveness on such a level; forgiveness means that I am saved from sinning and put into the Redeemer to grow up into His image. I am forgiven into a recreated relationship, i.e., into identification with God in Christ, so that the forgiven man is the holy man. The basis of human life is Redemption. There is nothing more certain in Time or Eternity than what Jesus Christ did on the Cross. He switched the whole of the human race back into right relationship to God, and any one of us can get into touch with God *now*, not presently.

Forgiveness is the miracle of grace; it is impossible for human beings to forgive, and it is because we do not see this that we misunderstand the revelation of forgiveness. The great characteristic of God is not that He says He will pay no more attention to what we have done, but that He forgives us, and in forgiving He is able to deal with our past, with our present and our future. Do I believe that God can deal with my 'yesterday' and make it as though it had never been? By means of the Redemption God undertakes to deal with a man's past, and He does it in two ways—first, He forgives it, and then He makes it a wonderful culture for the future. When God says 'Don't do that any more,' He instils into me the power that enables me not to do it any more, and the power comes by right of what Jesus Christ did on the Cross. That is the unspeakable wonder of the forgiveness of God, and when we become rightly related to God, we are to have the same relationship to our fellow men that God has to us. "And be ye kind one to another, tenderhearted, forgiving one another, even as God for Christ's sake hath forgiven you." (Ephesians iv. 32).

THE CALL OF GOD

Isaiah vi.

It is difficult to define the call of God—it is an implicit thing, like the call of the sea or of the mountains. Not everyone hears the call of the sea and of the mountains, but only those who have the nature of the sea or the mountains in them. In the same way no man hears the call of God unless he has the nature of God in him and has got into the way of listening to the implicit leading of the call. The significant thing is that God did not call Isaiah. There are times when God does call a man to a special work, but in Isaiah's case God did not call him; he 'overheard the voice of the Lord saying, Whom shall I send, and who will go for us?' Isaiah had been brought by spiritual concentration as well as consecration inside the moral frontiers where he could hear God's voice. We need trained ears to hear. One man may hear the call of God and another hear nothing; it depends on what goes on within the man, not outside him.

"In the year that king Uzziah died, I saw the Lord . . ." 'In the years of the great war, I saw the Lord'. . . That is the time when a man sees differently. It takes a crisis when the deeps are opened and life is profoundly altered before a man can say, 'I saw the Lord'. After Hezekiah had come face to face with death he said, "I shall go softly (as in solemn procession, R.V. marg.) all my years, because of the bitterness of my soul" (Isaiah xxxviii. 15). There is always a difference in the man who has come face to face with certain death, when he goes through the supreme crisis the true elements come out. This war has brought tension to countless lives and people are coming to see differently because of it. When a man goes through a crisis he fears he is losing God, but instead of that he is beginning to see Him for the first time, and he sees Him as a grander, more marvellous Being than ever he imagined.

I. Comprehensiveness of the Call.

The first thing that impresses us about the call of God is that it comes to the whole man, not to one part of him. The majority of us are godly in streaks, spiritual in sections; it takes a long time to locate us altogether to the call of God. We have special days and religious moods, but when we get into contact with God we are brought in touch with Reality and made all of a piece. Our Lord's life was all one reality, you could never cut it into two—shallow here and profound there. My conception of God must embrace the whole of my life. When I see the Lord truly I see Him as God of my whole being; if He is only God in sections of me, He is not God at all.

II. Consciousness of Grossness.

"Then said I, Woe is me! for I am undone; because I am a man of unclean lips, and I dwell in the midst of a people of unclean lips: for mine eyes have seen the King, the Lord of hosts." (v. 5).

Isaiah's words are a confession not of sin, but of the sense of absolute grossness. "I was as a beast before Thee" said the Psalmist, not an immoral beast but—'What an incapacitated type of man I am! I have seen the Lord, but how am I going to come anywhere near His marvellous holiness?' Any man will go to God for deliverance from sin, but it is another thing to have this consciousness of grossness dealt with; it takes discipline and patience and concentration. Will I agree that I am gross—'Woe is me! for I am undone'? If so, I am coming slowly to the condition Isaiah was in. It was his consciousness of grossness that brought Isaiah into a right relationship to God, that is an illuminating point. It is never my sense of goodness that brings me into touch with God, but my sense of unworthiness: 'Woe is me! for I am undone'—that brings me into the presence of God at once. When a man knows his destitution, knows he cannot get hold of God, cannot be the things he longs to be, he begins to realize what it was Jesus Christ came to do, viz., to supply what he really lacks.

108

There is no obstacle, nothing in the past or the present or in his heredity, that can stand in a man's way if he will only make room for Jesus Christ. Once let him realize his need—'I can't be holy, I can't be pure in heart, I can't be the child of my Father in heaven and be kind to the unthankful and evil, I can't love my enemies'—Jesus Christ claims that He can do all that for him, but it depends on the man, i.e., upon how much he has come up against the things he cannot do for himself.

III. CHARACTER OF THE COMMISSION.

Isaiah saw the Lord, then he saw himself; then he over-heard the voice of God saying "who will go?" and he said, "Here am I; send me"; and then God gave him a staggering message to deliver. "And He said, Go, and tell this people, Hear ye indeed, but understand not; and see ye indeed, but perceive not. Make the heart of this people fat, and make their ears heavy, and shut their eyes; lest they see with their eyes and hear with their ears, and understand with their heart, and turn again, and be healed" (vv. 9–10). 'Unless the people turn, the truth will deepen their condemnation, but you must speak.' God's condemnations as well as His promises are conditional; as long as we remain with the wrong disposition unremoved, every truth of God will harden us and ripen us for judgement.

Isaiah caught a sudden glimpse, terrible in its clearness, of his own sin and his people's sin. There is very little of that amongst us nowadays and a lot of gathering our spiritual skirts around us; instead of our repentance being social repentance and our intercession vicarious, we are vindictive and bitter in spirit. The sight of God deepens humiliation in a saint and lifts him into intercession. Repentance is needed not only for individual sins, but for social sins. There is a social repentance to-day, but it is repentance not for the honour of God but because of the sorrows and sufferings of the people. All through the Bible runs the idea of *national* repentance, of *social* sanctification, until the idea reaches its climax in *a holy city*.

109

SPIRITUAL DISENCHANTMENT AND DELIGHT

I. Disillusionment and the Furnace of Disappointment.

"Let no man glory in men. For all things are yours . . ."
(1 Corinthians iii. 21.)

Enchantment in the natural realm means to be taken out of your wits by song and rhythm; spiritual enchantment comes along the line of aggressive Christian work, meetings, and the contagion of other people's joy, and it is ensnaring. If we get taken up with salvation or with holiness or Divine healing instead of with Jesus Christ, we will be disillusioned. We pin our faith to a plan of salvation that can be expressed in words and we glory in it, then we begin to find it does not work and a curious disillusionment begins. It sounds all right, but its fruit is not that which bears a family likeness to Jesus Christ, and it causes us consternation if we are conscientious and desirous of being all that God wants us to be. Many a man to-day when he is dumped down in the desert has found disillusionment, he is amongst men who do not care for his religion, and he finds there is not the thrill and the joy there used to be; he realizes he has been fostering a religious life which is not genuine, and spiritual cynicism may be the result. A cynic spiritually is one who cuts himself off from other people because the enchantment of service and association with others instead of producing reality has been engendering priggishness, the attitude of a superior person. Paul continually warns 'Don't glory in men.' If you find your spiritual character is disappointing you, you are not developing a family likeness to Jesus Christ, it is because there is no inner reality. When you come to the furnace of disappointment, beware of the swing of the pendulum. Discouragement means the heart knocked out of self-love and my estimate of what God can do. We are also impatient with the things that are neither black nor white, but immensely difficult and perplexing, not easy to decipher. We are made up of a thousand and one springs and the only One who can bring the thing out right is the One who designed it. If a man has never gone through a spell of fanaticism it is because he is not prepared to cut off anything in order to get at reality. It is essential to be maimed for a while in order to develop our life with God (see Matthew v. 29-30).

II. DETACHMENT FROM THE FURY OF DESIRE.

"For by Him were all things created, . . . and He is before all things, and by Him all things consist." (Colossians i. 16-17).

Our natural life is a fury of desire for the things we can see. That is the meaning of lust—I must have it at once, a fury of desire without any regard for the consequences. I have to be detached from the things I can see and be brought into a living relationship with the Creator of those things. If I am taken up with the created things and forget Jesus Christ I shall find that things disappoint and I get disillusioned. If my body is 'bossed' by personal self-realization I am defiling the temple of the Holy Ghost; I may be moral and upright but I have become ruler over my own life. 'Give up your right to yourself to Me', says Jesus, 'let Me realize Myself in you.' He quenches the fury of desire by detaching us from things so that we may know Him. In this way God brings us into the fulness of life. The majority of us are not in the place where God can give us 'the hundredfold more'. We say, "A bird in the hand is worth two in the bush", while God is wanting to give us the bush with all the birds in it! It is necessary to be detached from things and then come back to them in a right relationship. A sense of property is a hindrance to spiritual growth, that is why so many of us know nothing about communion with Jesus Christ.

When we are detached from things on the inside the fury

111

of desire burns itself out. The attitude is not one born of external detachment, that is atheistic, Paul told Timothy to beware of 'those who teach abstinence from meats and marriage'. The detachment is not to be that of an æsthete but that which springs from being in perfect communion with God. Our Lord's external life was so social that the men of His day, who were externally detached, said of Him, 'Behold, a gluttonous man, and a winebibber'. They were detached externally, but not in spirit; Jesus Christ was detached in His disposition, but not externally. Those of us who are spiritual are hopelessly blind to God's purpose; the Spirit of God is all the time trying to make us detached in mind in order to bring us into real communion with God. God is trying to educate us in inner martyrdom and we won't have it, we get tired of being educated spiritually.

III. Devotion to the Face of Deity.

"Looking unto Jesus . . ." (Hebrews xii. 2).

If I want to see the Face of God I must fast from other things and concentrate on God. If in my inner life I am under apprehension by Jesus Christ for the time being I am out of touch with ordinary things. To fast is not to give up food, but to cut off the right arm, and pluck out the right eye. But that is only a stage, what we are tending towards is the perfection Jesus speaks of in Matthew v. 48— "Ye therefore shall be perfect, as your heavenly Father is perfect"; but in order to get there we have to go the longest way round. The end is a relationship to God perfect and complete in every particular, but it means going through a furnace of disillusionment, and the furnace burns hard. One of the cruellest experiences is the disappointment over what we find in other lives. The last thing we learn is not to glory in men. Jesus Christ never expected from human nature what it was not designed to give; consequently He was never bitter or cynical. Unless our human relationships are based in God they will end in frantic disillusionment. The cause of it is the demand in human nature for satisfaction. No human being can ever give satisfaction, and when I demand it and do not get it I become cruel and spiteful. When we are rightly related to Jesus Christ human love is transfigured because the last aching abyss of the heart is satisfied; but if the relationship with God is cut out our relationship to others is embittered. When once the relationship with God is right the satisfaction of human love is marvellous.

Christianity is not devotion to work, or to a cause, or a doctrine, but devotion to a Person, the Lord Jesus Christ. Christianity is a personal relationship which works spontaneously by 'the moral originality of the Holy Ghost', there is a perfect gaiety of delight. You could never awaken self-pity in the Apostle Paul, you might starve him or imprison him, but you could never knock out of him that uncrushable gaiety and certainty of God. A khamseen wind knocks us out! Paul refused to take anything or anyone seriously but Jesus Christ. That is Our Lord's teaching in the Sermon on the Mount, viz., 'Be carefully careless of everything saving your relationship to Me'. We take everything else but that seriously. Our experience of spiritual delight depends upon whether we are getting to know Jesus Christ better, whether we have the power to make what we know real. If you are going through disenchantment, remember that is not the end, the end is the life which exhibits the spirit of Jesus—"I delight to do Thy will, O My God."

HOW TO USE VICTORY

"And in the morning, rising up a great while before day, He went out and departed into a solitary place, and there prayed." (Mark i. 35).

This incident in the life of Our Lord occurred after what one would call a most successful day. He had endured the fierce onslaught in the wilderness, driven there for the devil to do his worst, and had come off more than conqueror, for we read that "angels came and ministered unto Him." If after a season of temptation a saint retains the power that draws the purest spirits to him, he may feel assured that the temptation has been gone through with successfully. Our Lord had called the men who were to be His disciples, and they had promptly left all and followed Him; He had had a triumphant time in Capernaum, casting out demons and setting men and women free. The fame and success of this mysterious Being grew, and we read that "all the city was gathered together at the door." It was after this time of eminent success in relieving men and blessing them that Jesus departed into a solitary place and spent the night in prayer.

Dr. George Adam Smith, in a sermon on Prayer, uses the following illustration from his own experience in Switzerland. He was an ardent mountain climber, and (I quote from memory) as he neared the top of a certain mountain his guide stepped back in order to let him have the privilege of being first on the top. He said the exhilaration of the experience made him leap and jump for joy, but instantly the guide called out, 'Down on your knees! It isn't safe standing up there.' Dr. Smith used the illustration in the way I want to use it. After our days of successful service are we spending too much time in exuberant joy and shouting, forgetting that the only safe place is on our knees?

"And in the morning, rising up a great while before day, He went out, and departed into a solitary place, and there prayed." I wonder what that night and early dawn hid? Our Lord went through His days with such easy power; what did He do in those solitary moments alone with God? Did He go back, in mind at least, to 'the glory which He had with the Father before the world was'? Did He recline on the bosom of the Father and hear unspeakable words not lawful to utter? Such thoughts as these are not presumptuous but the meditation of the heart that knows what communion with God means. If that communion means so much to a human heart that has been saved and sanctified through the Atonement, what must it have meant to the Son of God? What it was Our Lord experienced is hidden from us, yet we too in our measure have had the unspeakable experience, if rare, when the dark night of Nature gives place to the dawn, when the 'huge and thoughtful' silence of the night makes everything that is petty and trifling fall away, and lifts us into the larger isolation, which is no isolation but the realization of the presence of God.

Where do we place the night of prayer and the dawn of intercession in our soul's calendar? do we place it after a day of marvellous success in work for God? If we do not, our souls are in peril. Have we ever sufficiently realized our responsibility along the line of intercession? The Apostle Paul emphasizes the tremendous importance of prayer— "Praying always with all prayer and supplication in the Spirit, and watching thereunto with all perseverance and supplication for all saints; *and for me*, . . ." When our souls have been lifted into the presence of God and we have grasped some truth with new illumination, how much time have we spent in prayer for those servants and handmaids whom God has used to bless us? We allow ourselves to imagine that it would be presumptuous on our part to pray for the 'Pauls'; but this is a snare of Satan.

Notice this phrase, "He departed into a solitary place"; and notice also Our Lord's instructions regarding private prayer—"But thou, when thou prayest, enter into thy closet, *and when thou hast shut thy door*, pray to thy Father which is in secret." Any soul who has not that solitary place alone with God is in supreme peril spiritually. Let us ask ourselves if we have allowed the solitary places to be broken down or built over with altars that look beautiful, and people passing by say 'How religious that man or woman must be.' Such an altar, if there is no other in the solitary place, is an insult to the deep work of God in our souls. God grant we may learn more and more of the profound joy of getting alone with God in the dark of the night and toward the early dawn.

THE WITNESS OF SORROW

"Set a mark upon the foreheads of the men that sigh and that cry for all the abominations that be done in the midst thereof." (Ezekiel ix. 4).

We can fathom our own natures by the things we sorrow over. In this ancient Book of Ezekiel the man clothed in linen, with a writer's inkhorn by his side, was to set a mark upon the foreheads of the men who sorrowed for the city's sin. Let us take time to wonder if such a visitant on such an errand would mark us as among the people privileged to sorrow thus. Jeremiah has been called 'the weeping prophet', and in his Lamentations we find that the secret of his sorrow is Jerusalem, the city of his love. "How doth the city sit solitary, that was full of people!" (i. 1). Instantly our minds pass on to what is recorded in Luke xix. 41, "And when He drew nigh, He saw the city and wept over it," and we remember with adoring wonder that Our Lord is known throughout all generations as "a Man of sorrows."

WORLDLY SORROW.

". . . the sorrow of the world worketh death." (2 Corinthians vii. 10).

It is a terrible thing to say, and yet true, that there is a sorrow so selfish, so sentimental and sarcastic that it adds to the sin of the city. All sorrow that arises from being baffled in some selfish aim of our own is of the world and works death. Those who sorrow over their own weaknesses and sins and stop short at that, have a sorrow that only makes them worse, it is not a godly sorrow that works repentance. Oh that all men knew that every sentiment has its appropriate reaction, and if the nature does not embrace that reaction it degenerates into a sullen sentimentalism that kills all good action.

How certain it is that the men in Jerusalem of old upon whose foreheads the mark was set, were working out the appropriate reaction of their sorrow. It is an appalling thing

117

to mourn and sigh over the sins and iniquities of our city and do nothing about it.

WORKING SORROW.

"For godly sorrow worketh repentance unto a salvation which bringeth no regret:" (2 Corinthians vii. 10, R.V., marg.).

No one can be touched with sorrow for the sins of his city unless he has felt keen sorrow over his own sins. The Apostle Paul never forgot his past sins (see 1 Timothy i. 12–16). Scriptural repentance leads to positive salvation and sanctification; the only truly repentant man is the holy man. Every forgiven soul will love the world so much that he hates to death the sin that is damning men; to love the world in any other sense is to be "an enemy of God": to love the world as God loves it is to spend and be spent that men might be saved from their sins. Godly sorrow not only works a positive godliness, but grants us the mark of the Cross in winning souls, an unsleeping sorrow that keeps us at it night, day and night, "filling up that which is behind of the afflictions of Christ".

WINSOME SORROW.

"Behold, and see if there be any sorrow like unto my sorrow." (Lamentations i. 12).

The sign for the world without God is a circle, complete in and for itself; the sign for the Christian is the Cross. The Christian knows by bitter yet blessed conviction of sin that no man is sufficient for himself, and he thereby enters into identification with the Cross of Calvary, and he longs and prays and works to see the sinful, self-centred world broken up and made the occasion for the mighty Cross to have its way whereby men may come to God and God come down to men.

WEAKENING SORROW.

"What, could ye not watch with Me one hour?" (Matthew xxvi. 40).

118

"For this cause many among you are weak and sickly, and not a few sleep." (1 Corinthians xi. 30).

There are many to-day who are suffering from spiritual sleeping sickness, and the sorrow of the world which works death is witnessed in all directions. If personal sorrow does not work itself out along the appropriate line, it will lull us to a pessimistic sleep. For instance, when we see our brother 'sinning a sin not unto death' do we get to prayer for him, probed by the searching sorrow of his sin? (see 1 John v. 16). Most of us are so shallow spiritually that when Our Lord in answer to some outrageous request we have made, asks us— "Are ye able to drink the cup that I drink? or to be baptized with the baptism that I am baptized with?" we say "We are able." Then He begins to show us what the cup and the baptism meant to Him—"But I have a baptism to be baptized with; and how am I straitened till it be accomplished!" (Luke xii. 50). And Jesus said unto them, "Ye shall indeed drink of the cup that I drink of; and with the baptism that I am baptized withal shall ye be baptized"—and there begins to dawn for the disciple the great solemn day of martyrdom which closes for ever the day of exuberant undisciplined service, and opens the patient pilgrimage of pain and joy, with "more of the first than the last".

Without Sorrow.

Many are in the 'show business' spiritually, and the danger of this is greater than at first appears; it is a danger as old as the Book of Job, and is expressed in the character of Eliphaz who takes up the position of a superior person because of his own mysterious experience. Such an one could never have the mark set on his forehead as one who sighs and cries for the sin of his city; instead he would be an un-suffering dogmatist forgetting all about the sin of his city in his own personal experience. To-day there are in our midst many so-called Christian movements, but they bear the characteristic of being without sorrow for sin and without sympathy for suffering.

The witness of sorrow identifies us with Our Lord "who His

own self bare our sins in His body"; it binds us—if one may reverently put it so—into a mighty league of sin-bearers, pouring out the strenuous service of love and long-suffering akin to the love which God has shown to us. Thank God for the beauty of the Cross-crowned lives; it is the mark of the highest type of Christian life, the evidence of complete salvation.

And thus that far-off day in dim antiquity is linked with the great Day yet to be, of which it is written, "And they shall see His face; *and His name shall be in their foreheads.*" (Revelation xxi. 4).

SINCERITY AND REALITY

"Simon, I have somewhat to say unto thee. . . . Master, say on." (Luke vii. 40).

It is quite possible to be a sincere person, to be in earnest in proclaiming the truth of God, and yet not have one iota of reality along with it. This does not mean that the sincere person is a hypocrite or a sham, but it does mean that he has never understood that God wants him to be *real*.

In Luke vii. we read that "one of the Pharisees desired Him that He would eat with him. And He entered into the Pharisee's house, and sat down to meat." Simon, his host, was no doubt sincere; he kept his own counsel, and while he said nothing openly of his disapproval of the penitent woman's presence, yet he "spake within himself, saying, This man, if he were a prophet, would have perceived who and what manner of woman this is which toucheth Him, that she is a sinner." Then Jesus proved He was a prophet indeed by telling Simon aloud all he had been thinking silently, and went on to point out that his Pharisaic standards had caused him to treat Him in a neglectful manner— "thou gavest Me no water for My feet:" "thou gavest Me no kiss:" "My head with oil thou didst not anoint; . . ." When Our Lord enters our homes, or our churches, or social order, and says "I have somewhat to say unto thee," many of us, like Simon, answer quite sincerely, "Master, say on," although what Jesus has to say may prove just as unpalatable to us as it must have been to Simon.

Custom in spiritual matters is apt to make us peculiarly dead to much that Jesus Christ has to say—our perfectly sincere mood blinds us to the terrible fact that we are utterly un-real. What about all our sincere talk of sanctification— are we *really* sanctified? our sincere talk about the Holy Spirit—are we *really* indwelt by the Spirit? our sincere talk about the Sermon on the Mount—are we *really* living out its teaching? Let us examine ourselves and see whether

religious 'use and wont' has not resulted in our being perfectly sincere in our testimony for the Truth while we are
quite un-real as regards a genuine living out of the Truth.
We have to beware of the deadening of our conscience
spiritually through familiarity with certain favourite passages
of Scripture (e.g., Luke xi. 13, John iii. 16, Galatians ii. 20).
There is a kind of quiet smugness about a knowledge of
Scripture which says, sincerely, 'Thank God I know that
now,' while the life may be as un-real as a mirage, for 'the
letter killeth, but the Spirit alone gives life.'

It may give us a surprising shock to have our spiritual
customs broken into by some word of Jesus applied by the
Spirit, but in this way the sensitiveness of our conscience,
which is ever apt to go to sleep over the repetition of sincere
religious customs, is quickened. We may think it a great
thing to answer to Jesus, in all sincerity, "Master, say on,"
and yet it may piously mean that we only intend to listen
to Him about the things over which we have made up our
minds; it is quite a different matter to be willing, at all cost
to spiritual pride and prejudice, to be willing to re-arrange
everything under the authority of Jesus Christ, until we are
real with the vivid reality which tells not only in our actions,
but in the atmosphere we carry with us. May the Holy Spirit
keep us full of the marvel of the statements of Jesus, and
so renew us in the spirit of our minds that we more and more
sensitively apprehend God's purpose in our lives.

The cure for this perilous divorce between sincerity and
reality lies in the determined service of the mind. To say
"Master, say on" as a mere homage of the lips, while we are
quietly determined to go on just as we have always done,
is false and damaging, and this is bound to be the result
in the most sincere soul among us unless we allow the Holy
Spirit to continually renew our minds by concentration on
The Truth. It is the spiritual interpretation of Our Lord's
teaching which makes us real, and gives us the power to
overcome the world and be the inspirers of many a lagging-
behind soul. The strength of a *real* man or *real* woman
cannot be estimated. There is always a great danger that

the sentimental emotions which drift around every high and holy certainty may shift us from the courageous concentration on Christ's teaching which alone can make us and keep us real.

Let us with renewed concentration so obey Our Lord that He may find us hopeful, alert, wide-awake saints, determined to keep in sympathy with His words and His point of view.

". . . I have somewhat to say unto *thee. . . . Master, say on.*"

DEVOTIONAL 'WE' OR 'ME'?

'WE' meant to serve so much,
In daily life to help the poor and sad,
And by the tenderness of word and deed
To make them feel God's goodness, and be glad;
    Should 'I' serve less?

'WE' meant to love so much,
To let our kindred, friends and neighbours feel
That we had been with Christ and learned of Him
The gentlest ways of love to help and heal;
    Dare 'I' love less?

Because 'WE' meant so much,
Shall I with coward heart lie down and see
Life's meaning and its service unfulfilled?
My Father! Grant the strength and love to 'me'
    Not to do less!

Matthew xxiii. 8–10

The aspect of collective discipleship and individual discipleship is frequently brought out in the New Testament. It is so easy to talk about what 'we' are going to do—'we' are going to do marvellous things, and it ends in none of us doing anything. The incident in John vi. 66–71 brings clearly to light the 'we' aspect as emphasized by Peter, and also Our Lord's rigorous sorting of it out to the personal element—"Would ye also go away? Simon Peter answered Him, Lord, to whom shall we go? . . ." Then Jesus says something that seems irrelevant but is not—"Did I not choose you the twelve, and one of you is a devil?" We never become disciples in crowds or even in twos; discipleship is always a personal matter (see Luke xiii. 23–4; John xxi. 21–2). We are brought together by God, not by our own selecting. Let me get my 'me' rightly related to Jesus Christ and I shall find others will get related in the same way.

I. OMNISCIENT TEACHER.

"For one is your Teacher, and all ye are brethren."

It is necessary to haul ourselves up short and ask—Do I recognise Jesus Christ as my Teacher, or am I at the mercy of vague spiritual impulses of my own? Am I accepting someone else's conception of God, or am I bringing everything I hear, every impulse, every emotion that comes to me, into line with the teaching of Christ? The test of every spiritual impulse is, does it make Jesus Christ the supreme Teacher? Jesus said, "When the Holy Spirit is come, He shall teach you all things." The Holy Spirit is the great bond of union because He keeps us united to the one Teacher. Jesus Christ is not a great Teacher alongside Plato and other great teachers; He stands absolutely alone. "Test your teachers," said Jesus; the teachers who come from God are those who clear the way to Jesus Christ, and keep it clear. We are estimated in God's sight as workers by whether or not we clear the way for people to see Jesus.

II. OMNIPRESENT FATHER.

"For one is your Father, which is in heaven."

George MacDonald in one of his books gives a graphic description of the wonderful simplicity a child of God has; he pictures Job opening God's private door, as it were, and flinging himself into His presence and presenting his problems. He is indicating the freedom a child of God has to come and say, 'I am puzzled by this and that; why should things be so?' He is coming not to a monarch who will terrify him, but to a Father, if he is a disciple, and he can speak just like a child with perfect simplicity and freedom. Some of us seem to have the idea that we are away in a howling wilderness and we must cry and agonize before we can get God's ear. Turn to the New Testament and see what Jesus says—"Father, I thank Thee that Thou hast heard Me. And I knew that Thou hearest Me always."

"One is your Father"—your Father! Think for one minute, have you behaved to-day as though God were your Father or have you to hang your head in absolute shame before Him for the miserable, mean, unworthy thoughts you have had about your life? It all springs from one thing, you have lost hold of the idea that God is your Father. Some of us are such fussy, busy people, refusing to look up and realize the tremendous revelation in Jesus Christ's words—"*Your heavenly Father knoweth . . .*"

III. Omnipotent Master.

"For one is your Master, even Christ."

There is no room in Our Lord's conception of discipleship for a disciple to say, 'Now, Lord, I am going to serve You.' That does not come into His idea of discipleship. It is not that we work for God, but that God works through us; He uses us as He likes, He allots our work where He chooses, and we learn obedience, even as our Lord did. ". . . though He were a Son, yet learned He obedience by the things which He suffered." Jesus said, "As the Father hath sent Me, even so send I you." How did God send Jesus? To do His will. How does Jesus send His disciples? To do His will. "Ye shall be My witnesses," a satisfaction to Christ wherever we are placed.

"One is your Master, even Christ"; He is all-wise, stand true to Him and other saints will be true to you; if you stand true to someone else's teaching you will find you become segregated from the saints. "But if we walk in the light, as He is in the light, we have fellowship one with another, . . ." If you hide anything in your life with God, down you go, no matter what you have experienced; hide nothing.

THE MINISTRY OF THE INTERIOR

"I have set watchmen upon thy walls, O Jerusalem; they shall never hold their peace day nor night: ye that are the Lord's remembrancers, take ye no rest, and give Him no rest, till He establish, and till He make Jerusalem a praise in the earth." (Isaiah lxii. 6–7).

"And the Lord said unto him, Go through the midst of the city, through the midst of Jersalem, and set a mark upon the foreheads of the men that sigh and cry for all the abominations that be done in the midst thereof." (Ezekiel ix. 4).

Do I know anything experimentally about this aspect of things? Have I ever spent one minute before God in intercessory importunity over the sins of other people? If we take these statements of the prophets and turn the searchlight on ourselves, we will be covered with shame and confusion because of our miserably selfish, self-centred Christianity.

How many of us have ever entered into this Ministry of the Interior where we become identified with Our Lord and with the Holy Spirit in intercession? It is a threefold inter-cession: at the Throne of God, Jesus Christ; within the saint, the Holy Ghost; outside the saint, common-sense circum-stances and common-sense people, and as these are brought before God in prayer the Holy Spirit gets a chance to make intercession according to the will of God. That is the meaning of personal sanctification, and that is why the barriers of personal testimony must be broken away and effaced by the realization of why we are sanctified—not to be fussy workers for God, but to be His servants, and this is the work, vicarious intercession.

One of the first lessons learnt in the Ministry of the Interior is to talk things out before God in soliloquy—tell Him what you know He knows in order that you may get to know it as He does. All the harshness will go and the suffering sadness of God's Spirit will take its place, and gradually you will be brought into sympathy with His point of view.

There is an advocacy of holiness which was never born at Calvary, it is the resuscitation of the Pharisaic spirit dressed in the garb of Pentecost—an insufferable superiority. The Spirit of God must have a deep indignation at the preaching of holiness that is not the holiness of Jesus. The holiness of Jesus is the most humble thing on earth.

When God puts a weight on you for intercession for a soul don't shirk it by talking to him. It is much easier to talk to him than to talk to God about him—much easier to talk to him than to take it before God and let the weight crush the life out of you until gradually and patiently God lifts the life out of the mire. That is where very few of us go.

When God brings a burden to you never allow it to develop into carnal suspicion. In the Ministry of the Interior all we have to do is simply to take the matter before God and be made 'crushed grapes' until the Holy Spirit produces such an atmosphere that the one who is wrong cannot endure it. That is God's method, and we interfere by using our own discernment.

The knowledge of where people are wrong is a hindrance to prayer, not an assistance. 'I want to tell you of the difficulties so that you may pray intelligently.' The more you know the less intelligently you pray because you forget to believe that God can alter the difficulties.

"Howbeit when the Son of man cometh, shall He find faith on the earth?" Which one of us would God stop at and say, 'That one is My remembrancer'? or would He have to say, 'That one is serving a conviction of his own, he is not My servant at all'?

". . . greater works than these shall he do; because I go unto the Father. *And whatsoever ye shall ask in My name, that will I do.*"

"FOR CHRIST'S CROWN AND COVENANT"

This motto of the Scottish Covenanters comes nearer to the New Testament conception of loyalty to Christ than any other all down the centuries of Christianity, and what we need to do is to translate it into terms which fit our own day and generation.

I. LOYALTY TO HIS ROYALTY.

"Pilate therefore said unto Him, Art Thou a king then? Jesus answered, Thou sayest it, because I am a king." (John xviii. 37—R.V., marg.).

Jesus Christ is not only Saviour, He is King, and He has the right to exact anything and everything from us at His own discretion. We talk about the joys and comforts of salvation; Jesus Christ talks about taking up the cross and following Him. Whenever Our Lord talks about discipleship He prefaces it with an 'If'—'you need not unless you like'. It is always easier in certain crises to be 'Demas' than a devoted disciple. Very few of us know anything about loyalty to Jesus Christ. "For My sake"—that is what makes the iron saint. We look upon Jesus Christ as the best Example of the Christian life; we do not conceive of Him as Almighty God Incarnate, with all power in heaven and on earth. We make Him a comrade, One who in the battle of life has more breath than the rest of us and He turns round to lend a hand. We deal with Him as if He were one of ourselves; we do not take off the shoes from our feet when He speaks. Jesus Christ is Saviour, and He saves us into His own absolute and holy lordship.

II. LOYALTY TO HIS LORDSHIP.

"Ye call Me, Master, and Lord: and ye say well, for so I am." (John xiii. 13).

From a dog to a man, the master makes the difference.

'Pi' people have no master, they are always hole-and-corner folks. Whenever a man is mastered by Jesus Christ you have a man "with breast and back as either should be", no whimperer, no sentimentalist, no pietist, but a man of God. That can only be produced by the mastership of Jesus Christ. The curious thing about Our Lord is that He never insists on our obedience. When we begin to usurp authority and say, 'You must' and 'you shall' it is a sure sign that we are out of touch with the supreme Authority. If you are in a position of authority and people are not obeying you, the greatest heart-searching you can have is the realization that the blame does not lie with them, but with you; there is a leakage going on spiritually. Get right with God yourself, and every other one will get in touch with God through you.

III. LOYALTY TO HIS RULE.

"I am crucified with Christ: nevertheless I live; yet not I, but Christ liveth in me." (Galatians ii. 20).

To imagine that Jesus Christ came to save and sanctify *me* is heresy: He came to save and sanctify me *into Himself*, to be His absolute bondslave; so completely His bondslave that when He speaks there is no possibility of dispute. 'I reckon on you for extreme service, with no complaining on your part and no explanation on Mine.' We begin to debate and say, 'Why shouldn't I do this? I'm within my rights.' That idea is so foreign to Our Lord's conception that He has made no provision for it. The passion of Christianity is that I deliberately sign away my own rights and become a bondslave of Jesus Christ. Any fool can insist on his rights, and any devil will see that he gets them; but the Sermon on the Mount means that the only right the saint will insist on is the right to give up his rights. That is the New Testament idea of sanctification, and that is why so few get anywhere near the baptism with the Holy Ghost. 'I want to be baptized with the Holy Ghost so that I may be of use'—then it is all up. We are baptized with the Holy
130

Ghost not *for* anything at all, but entirely, as Our Lord puts it, to be His witnesses, those with whom He can do exactly what He likes.

IV. LOYALTY TO HIS CALLING.

"And we know that to them that love God all things work together for good, even to them that are called according to His purpose." (". . . God worketh all things with them for good."—R.V., marg.) (Romans viii. 28).

It is only the loyal saint who believes that God engineers circumstances. We take such liberties with our circumstances, we treat the things that happen as if they were engineered by men, although we say that we believe God engineers them. To be faithful in every circumstance means that we have only one loyalty, and that is to our Lord. Most of us are too devoted to our own ideas of what God wants even to hear His call when it comes. We may be loyal to what we like, but we may find we have been disloyal to God's calling of us by not recognizing Him in either the distress and humiliation or the joy and blessing. The test of loyalty always comes just there.

Loyalty to our own ideas is always the result of disloyalty to a person. God educates us by people. Any refusal to be loyal to whatever 'Elijah' God sends us is detected by pious talk about being loyal to a word of God. Loyalty to the teachers God sends ends ultimately in supreme devotion to Himself. Beware how you treat the messengers of God because there is only one aim in the true messengers of God, and that is unflinching loyalty to the Lordship of Jesus Christ, and we shall have to account to God for our heedfulness of them or our heedlessness.

CLEANSED FROM SIN

I. Where Sin Ceases. *'Walk in the Light.'*

"But if we walk in the light, as He is in the light, we have fellowship one with another, and the blood of Jesus Christ His Son cleanseth us from all sin" (1 John i. 7).

". . . as He is in the light"—God has nothing to hide: have I anything to hide from God? If I try to vindicate myself, I am not in the light; if I say 'I can explain that away,' I am not in the light, I have something to cover up; but if I walk in the light *as God is in the light*, then comes the amazing revelation that "the blood of Jesus Christ His Son cleanseth us from all sin," so that God Almighty can see nothing to censure in me. That is not a conscious experience, it is a revelation. If you make the experience of conscious freedom from sin the test you make hypocrites. Sin enough and you will soon be unconscious of sin. The nature of sin is that it destroys the possibility of knowing that you sin. Sin ceases when I am in the light as God is in the light, and in no other way. In my experience it works with a keen poignant knowledge of what sin is (cf. 1 Timothy i. 15–16).

"If we confess our sins, He is faithful and just to forgive us our sins, and to cleanse us from all unrighteousness" (1 John i. 9). Watch the difference between *confessing* and *admitting*; the majority of us are quite ready to admit, it is the rarest thing to get to the place where we will confess— confess to God, not to man. It is much more difficult to confess to God than we are apt to think. It is not confessing in order to be forgiven; confession is the evidence that I am forgiven. God does not forgive me because I confess; I realize by my confession that I am forgiven. Am I willing to be brought to the place where God draws out my confession? When the Spirit of God convicts of sin it is not like a detective convicting a criminal, it is sin finding out a man's own nature and making him say, 'Yes, I recognize it.' When once your sin does find you out, the exquisite pain of confessing acts like the sweetest medicine—"a broken and a contrite heart, O God, Thou wilt not despise." Beware of having anything that makes your mind accept an excuse for yourself. I can step out of darkness into the light—when God is willing? No, when I am willing. 'I do want to be in living communion with God'; I don't, if I did, I could be there in one second; the reason I am not there is that I won't confess, I won't submit to God's condemnation of the thing. Immediately confession is made the Atonement of Our Lord steps in with its supernatural efficacy.

II. WHERE LOVE INVADES. *'Walk in Love.'*

"And walk in love, even as Christ also loved you, . . ." (Ephesians v. 2).

If I want God's light to increase in me until I am a child of the light, 1 Corinthians xiii. is what I must measure up to.

"Love suffereth long, and is kind:" Have you had to suffer anything? have you remained kind in heart? It is damnably easy to be kind in speech and cruel in heart. To 'walk in love' means that the very breathing of my disposition is kindness. If I get the trick of the right expression of face and speech, I can harbour a spirit that is as unlike Jesus Christ as can be. Beware of affectation spiritually, it is the very paw of the devil over the saint.

"Love envieth not;" Envy and jealousy may remain entirely latent until competition is launched on a certain plane and I recognize someone else's superiority; there is no getting away from it, I recognize that in the particular quality on which I prided myself, the other person is superbly my superior. How do I know when I am envious, jealous of someone being what I am not? When I am secretly rather glad, though my lips say the opposite, when that one stumbles. It springs from a jealous dislike of easily recognized superiority in the very same line of things as my own. No one can be with a superior person without having a feeling

of envy and jealousy unless he is a saint; the saint knows no jealousy or envy because the life of the Lord Jesus is being manifested in him.

"seeketh not her own," Self is so completely effaced that the only characteristic of the life is, "in all the world, my God, there is none but thee." Its self does not bother its self, it is altogether devoted to God's interests in others.

"is not provoked," Was Jesus Christ ever irritable? am I? God will put me in places where it would be natural for me to be provoked so that He might magnify His grace in me.

"taketh not account of evil;" If someone has done an unkind thing to you, don't let it blot God out. Apart from God we do reckon with evil, we reason from that standpoint. To 'take no account of evil' does not mean we are ignorant of its existence; it means we do not take it in as a calculable factor. When the love of God is shed abroad in my heart by the Holy Ghost there is no lurking nest of remembrance in my spirit for the evil. Always beware of suspicion, it comes from the devil and ends there. The Holy Spirit never suspects.

1 Corinthians xiii. is sentiment transfigured into character. Love springs spontaneously, that is, it is not premeditated; but love does not develop like that. Both naturally and spiritually love requires careful developing; love won't stay if it is not sedulously cultivated. If I am not careful to keep the atmosphere of my love right by cultivation, it will turn to lust—'I must have this thing for myself.' No love of the natural heart is safe unless the human heart has been satisfied by God first. The tragedies of human lives can only be solved by an understanding of the one great fundamental truth that Jesus Christ alone can satisfy the last aching abyss of the human heart.

LEAST IN THE KINGDOM OF HEAVEN

"Whosoever therefore shall break one of these least commandments, and shall teach men so, he shall be called the least in the kingdom of heaven" (Matthew v. 19).

John Wesley in expounding this passage said it meant that 'whosoever shall break one of these least commandments, and shall teach men so, shall not be in the kingdom of heaven at all'; but Our Lord is warning that it is possible to be as 'the least' in the kingdom of heaven. When the apostle Paul says he is 'less than the least of all saints', he is not referring to this standard of measurement, but to himself in his own eyes. (*See* Ephesians iii. 8.)

What is it exactly to be 'least in the kingdom of heaven'? For one thing, the words surely point out the necessity of searching the Scriptures in order to find out what the commandments and precepts of God are. As we go on in the spiritual life the Spirit of God educates us down to the scruple, that is, He applies the commandments of God to all the ramifications of our being. We may see Christian people doing things that surprise us, and yet it would be untrue to say they were not Christians; as you watch their development in the ways of God you find they are becoming more and more careful over things they used to be careless over.

The writer to the Hebrews warns us about 'the sin which doth closely cling to us,' literally, the spirit of the age, the spirit which makes our minds obtuse to the commandments of God. There is a culture in the spiritual life not realized by all teachers and preachers, consequently they tell men that God does not hold certain things necessary. What an awakening awaits all such when they stand before God and find they have not glorified Him as they should have done, because they stood more for their own personal freedom and independent rights than for the careful searching out of Our Lord's commandments and teaching men regarding them. It is easy for those who are 'out and out' for God to condemn such teachers and put them outside the kingdom; Our Lord puts them not outside, but as 'least in the kingdom.'

This warning should bring us to the place where we measure up and see whether we are growing in sensitiveness towards all God's commandments so that we tremble at the very approach of any defilement that might blur the clear vision of His truth. Our spiritual fighting trim becomes enervated by any compromise with the world's standards, and if we teach men by both word and precept to do the same, we run perilously near being those Our Lord warns.

To know how to maintain and develop the habits of the holy life according to the commandments of God is the sublime education of the soul. There are times of ignorance that God 'winks at' and overlooks, but there are other times when He holds us responsible for being frivolous and light regarding His commandments. I wonder how many of us in our dealing with our fellow men have made it easy for them to break some of the commandments of God because it was so hard for us to appear unsympathetic with them? 'he shall be called least in the kingdom of heaven,' says Our Lord. What need there is that the minister of the Gospel should continually face himself with his Saviour, to know how he stands before Him, lest he fail to measure up to His standard, and having preached to others should himself become a castaway.

The argument that the keeping of certain commandments is not essential to salvation is such a mean, beggarly line of argument that it need scarcely be mentioned. If my love for God is so faint and poor that I will only do what is absolutely essential and not what it is my privilege to do, it is then that I deserve not only to be 'least in the kingdom of heaven,' but not to be in it at all. May every faculty of heart and mind and soul be roused up to be its glorious best for God all the time for the glory of the Lord Jesus Christ.

PAUL'S WAYS IN CHRIST

"For this cause have I sent unto you Timothy, . . . who shall put you in remembrance of my ways which be in Christ" (1 Corinthians iv. 17).

You say—'How can I follow Paul? I was not trained at the feet of Gamaliel like he was; nor have I any of his great gifts.' Watch Paul's argument in this very chapter—"For who maketh thee to differ from another? and what hast thou that thou didst not receive?" (v. 7.) The following has nothing to do with natural gifts, or natural ability, or natural anything; Paul says, 'Follow my ways *which be in Christ.*'

I. THE WAY OF CONVERSION.

"And he said, Who art Thou, Lord?" (Acts ix. 5).

When God touches a life by bereavement, or by sickness or disaster, it is always a supernatural touch. What did you do in that moment when the true attitude of your life was revealed in a flash? did you say with Saul of Tarsus, 'Who art Thou, Lord?' It was not the supernatural light from heaven that made Paul tremble, but the voice that spoke to him, the voice of the despised Nazarene: "I am Jesus whom thou persecutest: . . . And he trembling and astonished said, Lord, what wilt Thou have me to do?" Paul was turned in one second from a strong-willed intense Pharisee into a humble devoted slave of the Lord Jesus. There was no mention of sin, that came later; it was a complete surrender to the lordship of Jesus.

II. THE WAY OF CONSECRATION.

"For I will shew him how great things he must suffer for My name's sake." (Acts ix. 16).

There has been an absolute swing round in Saul's life, he has enthroned Jesus as Lord, and now Ananias comes and calls him 'Brother Saul', and mentions again *"the Lord, even Jesus that appeared unto thee in the way as thou camest, hath sent me, that thou mightest receive thy sight, and be filled with the Holy Ghost."* When Paul received his sight, he received a spiritual insight into the Person of Jesus Christ. Martin Luther said that Paul was intoxicated with Jesus Christ; He was never out of his waking or his sleeping moments, and all through his Epistles is stamped this certainty of his knowledge of Jesus as Lord. That is the marvellous thing about the baptism of the Holy Ghost, every other spell is gone—

'Since mine eyes have looked on Jesus
I've lost sight of all beside.'

The baptism of the Holy Ghost makes us witnesses to Jesus, not witnesses to what He can do, that is an elementary witness, but 'witnesses unto Me'. The spirit that comes in is not that of *doing* anything for Jesus, but of being a perfect delight to Him. "For I will show him how great things he must suffer *for My name's sake.*" Paul gloried in his suffering, and when he sums it all up he calls it 'our light affliction'! It is the triumphant phrase of a super-conqueror. You can't imagine Paul saying 'I've had such a tussle with the devil but I have got the victory'; it was the Victor who had got Paul, he was absolutely Jesus Christ's.

III. The Way of Conference.

"But when it pleased God, to reveal His Son in me; immediately I conferred not with flesh and blood:" (Galatians i. 15–16).

When Paul realized the Divine call he did not confer with flesh and blood, his own or any one else's; imagine him in the desert alone with God, while the Holy Ghost worked in him those revelations which found expression afterwards in his Epistles, and you have a picture of his way of conference. When God speaks to you what do you do? go to the nearest saint and ask him about it? That is wrong. If God has spoken, confer with Him alone, rely on the Holy Spirit, and He will soon clinch the matter. "My sheep hear My voice", said Jesus. Many go astray because they will not take Paul's way of conference. Born-again souls should be thrust out to testify, not into work; they need to soak before God until they become rooted and grounded in the revelation

138

of God, and have learned how to submit their will and intelligence to Jesus Christ.

IV. THE WAY OF CONFIDENCE.

"Though I might also have confidence in the flesh:" (Philippians iii. 4).

If any man has reason to boast in the flesh, Paul says he is that man—"an Hebrew of the Hebrews; as touching the law, a Pharisee; concerning zeal, persecuting the church; touching the righteousness which is in the law, blameless;" but, he says, we are those who "rejoice in Christ Jesus, and have no confidence in the flesh." Paul continually counsels, 'Don't glory in men.' The best of men are but the best of men. Never trust the best man or woman you ever met, trust only the Lord Jesus. If when you are sanctified you turn for one second to the natural life, the sentence of death is there. Never take your guidance from the natural life, but learn to sacrifice the natural to the will of God.

V. THE WAY OF THE CROSS.

"But none of these things move me, neither count I my life dear unto myself, . . ." (Acts xx. 24).

Does that sound like the modern advice—'Now do be careful, don't work so hard, you must look after yourself.' Paul says there is only one dear element about his life, and that is that it can be used for Jesus Christ to be glorified in. 'I keep under my body', he says; 'it does not dictate to me'. Paul had received a ministry from the Lord Jesus, and in comparison of accomplishing that, he held nothing else of any account. "He shall testify of Me before kings", and Paul did so in the most fearless manner. Paul is so bound up with what he preaches that you cannot separate his preaching from his testimony. His Epistles are a testimony that he is determined to know nothing among men save Jesus Christ, and Him crucified. He welcomed heartbreaks, tribulation, suffering, for one reason only, that these things kept him in unmoved devotion to the gospel of the grace of God.

God grant that being put in remembrance of Paul's ways in Christ, we may learn to follow those ways, to His glory.

DISCIPLESHIP

"Christ ruined many careers and brought sorrow and death to many souls." (*Dr. Forsyth.*)

I. THE CALL TO DISCIPLESHIP.

"If any man would come after Me, let him deny himself, and take up his cross daily, and follow Me " (Luke ix. 23).

The call of Jesus to discipleship has a fascinating side but also a desolating side; we nearly always ignore that side of the call. There is a difference between being a disciple and being what is called 'saved.' It is not the bad things that are the stumbling-block to becoming a disciple, anyone will give up sin and wrong if he knows how to, but will I give up the 'rightest' thing I have got, viz., my right to myself? will I crown Jesus as Lord? Whenever Our Lord talks about discipleship that is what He bases it on, the giving up of my right to myself—". . . *let him deny himself.*" 'Many are called, but few prove the choice ones', that is, few of us take up the cross and follow Jesus, the reason being not that we are irreligious and bad, but we don't prefer that Jesus should be Lord. We like to hear about deliverance from hell and forgiveness of sins, but this comes a bit too close, this demands too much, and we back out. "Upon this many of His disciples went back and walked no more with Him", they went back from following Jesus and never became actual disciples. If I do become a disciple my career may have to be ruined, am I prepared for it? is He worth it? "IF any man would come after Me . . ." 'If' means, 'You don't need to unless you like, but you won't be of any account to Me in this life unless you do'. Wherever Christian experience is proving unsatisfactory it is because the Holy Spirit is still battling around this one point, my right to myself, and until that is deliberately given over by me to Jesus Christ I will never have the relationship to Him He asks for.

II. THE COMMUNION OF DISCIPLESHIP.

"Rabbi, where abidest Thou? . . . Come, and ye shall see " (John i. 38, 40).

There is something so natural and yet so supernatural about Jesus. We never read that Jesus button-holed any-body; these men came to Him and asked, 'Master, where do you live?' He said 'Come, and ye shall see'—obvious and simple, yet full of Divine power. The difference between the Christianity stamped by the Holy Ghost and that stamped by ecstasy and fanaticism is just here, the one makes the supernatural 'spooky' and puts the natural nowhere; the other makes the supernatural natural. Jesus does not come to men in extraordinary ways, but in the most ordinary things—washing disciples' feet; preparing breakfast; at a wedding feast. The early disciples were not attracted to Jesus because of their sense of sin, they were religious men, in touch with the elemental forces of nature, simple and unconventional, and when they saw Jesus their spirit indicated at once—'This is the very One we have been looking for'. There are plenty of men who have not lived lives of sin—has Jesus Christ any message for them?

III. THE CROWN OF DISCIPLESHIP.

"John indeed did no miracle; but all things that John spake of this man were true." (John x. 41).

The crown of John's discipleship was that his disciples became the disciples of Jesus. 'And the two disciples heard John speak, and they followed Jesus' (John i. 37). If in the final issue the souls of those I have taught do not turn to Jesus when they see Him, I have been a traitor. In the New Testament it is never the personality of the preacher that counts, what counts is whether he knows how to direct those who come to him to Jesus. If a man preaches on the ground of his personality he is apt to be a detractor from Jesus. The only reason for presenting Jesus is that He is All-in-all to me absolutely. Many of us only know devoteeness to a creed, to a phase of evangelical truth, very few know anything about personal devotion to Jesus.

The call to discipleship comes as mysteriously as being born from above; once a man hears it, it profoundly alters everything. It is like the call of the sea, the call of the mountains, not everyone hears these calls, only those who have the nature of the sea or the mountains—and then only if they pay attention to the call. To hear the call of God or the call to discipleship necessitates education in understanding and discernment. Never be afraid of the thing that is vague, the biggest things in life are vague as far as expression goes, but they are realities.

"Go ye therefore, and make disciples of all the nations, . . ."—not 'Go out and save souls', but 'Go and *make disciples*'. It is comparatively easy to proclaim salvation from sin, but Jesus comes and says, 'What about you—if *you* would be My disciple, deny yourself, take up that cross daily, and follow Me.' It has nothing to do with eternal salvation, it has everything to do with our temporal value to God, and most of us do not care anything about our temporal worth to God, all we are concerned about is being saved from hell and put right for heaven. There is something infinitely grander than that, and Jesus Christ gives us a marvellous chance of giving up our right to ourselves to Him in order that we might become the devoted bondslaves of the One who saves us so supernaturally.

THE WORKER'S WAY ABOUT FAITH

I. FAITH AND THE ANCIENT WITNESS.

". . . And these all, having had witness borne to them through their faith . . ." (Hebrews xi. 4–40).

Faith is never defined; it is described, as in Hebrews xi. 1, but never defined. Definitions can only be given of things that are perfectly understood and are inferior to the mind that defines them. It is absurd to try and put God into a definition; if I can define God I am greater than God. Intellectual definition is of no use whatever in the spiritual life. Faith cannot be intellectually defined; faith is the inborn capacity to see God behind everything, the wonder that keeps you an eternal child. What is your faith to you—a wonderful thing, or a bandbox thing? Satisfaction is too often the peace of death; wonder is the very essence of life. Beware always of losing the wonder, and the first thing that stops wonder is religious conviction. Whenever you give a trite testimony the wonder is gone. The only evidence of salvation or sanctification is that the sense of wonder is developing, not at things as they are, but at the One who made them as they are. There is no set definition of faith into which you can fit these men and women, they were heroes of faith because they "endured, as seeing Him who is invisible." The acts of faith the writer refers to were not performed by astute-minded men and women who made defined statements about God, they were not tortured for convictions' sake, but for the sake of their faith. There is no mention of salvation from sin, the one point insisted on is their faith, and God is training us to do what they did, viz., live a life of tenacious hold upon God in spite of everything that happens. Do we know anything about this life of confidence in God, or are we everlastingly hunting in our theological 'wardrobes' for definitions to work to? Faith is the indefinable certainty of God behind everything, and is the one thing the Spirit of God makes clearer and clearer as we go on.

II. FAITH AND THE ABIDING WITNESS.

". . . looking unto Jesus, the author and finisher of (our) faith." (Hebrews xii. 2).

The abiding Witness is our Lord Jesus Christ, and the writer gives three characteristics of His life—*joy, renunciation*, and *reward*. The first element in the life of faith is joy, which means the perfect fulfilment of that for which we were created. Joy is not happiness; there is no mention in the Bible of happiness for a Christian, but there is plenty said about joy—". . . that they might have My joy fulfilled in themselves", said Jesus. The next element is the realisation that we have the delight of giving our lives as a love-gift to Jesus Christ. "He that loseth his life *for My sake* shall find it." Reward is the ultimate delight of knowing that God has fulfilled His purpose in my life; it is not a question of resting in satisfaction, but the delight of being in perfect conscious agreement with God.

III. FAITH AND THE ALERT WITNESS.

". . . let us also, . . . lay aside every weight, and the sin which doth so easily beset us, and let us run with patience the race that is set before us, . . ." (Hebrews xii. 1–3).

Run light—nothing clings to us more closely than trying to live up to the ideas we have got from saintly people. We have nothing to do with saintly people, we have only to do with 'looking to Jesus.' How much 'cargo' are you carrying in the upper storey? how many definitions to fit your teaching into? No wonder people have nervous breakdowns! Avoid definitions as you would avoid the devil. Immediately your mind accepts a definition you will learn no more about that thing until the definition is smashed. Definition and human authority are the two things that kill faith; with Jesus Christ there are no definitions at all. Jesus

144

Christ always taught vaguely; in the beginning of our Christian life we think He teaches definitely, and we get hold of trite definitions until we find the marvellous life of God is not there at all. *Run looking*—Keep nothing in view but the vision of the Lord Jesus Christ. To rest in any experience apart from Him, even though He gave it you, is to be away from the main Centre. Jesus Christ is first, second and third; let the revelation of His life keep you full of wonder, love and praise. *Run learning*—"Despise not the chastening of the Lord, nor faint when thou art rebuked of Him:". Never stop learning. People stagnate, not through backsliding, but because they stop learning and harden into a wrong mental poise. We learn through chastisement, because God is supplying heaven with sons and daughters, not with precious stones. Sons and daughters must grow, and God is never in a hurry with us. As you go on in the life of faith you find everything is becoming so simple that you are afraid it can't be true, it is so unlike what you had been taught. Beware of being in bondage to yourself or to other people. Oppression and depression never come from the Spirit of God. He never oppresses, He convicts and comforts. It is unconscious stubbornness that brings us into bondage. In the presence of Jesus we find how perverse and timid and unfaithful we have been, when God was going to enlarge our life we shrank back. The summing up of the life of faith is the teaching of Jesus in the Sermon on the Mount—*Be carefully careless about everything saving your relationship to God.*

.

THE CERTAINTIES OF THE KINGDOM

I. THE SUBSTRATUM OF CERTAINTY.

"Whom therefore ye ignorantly worship, Him declare I unto you . . .: for in Him we live, and move, and have our being;" (Acts xvii. 22–29).

Substratum—an under stratum or layer, a fundamental element that does not appear, but on which all that does appear rests.

There is a difference between the Christian foundation and my experience of it. I can no more experience the foundation of my faith than a building can experience its foundation; but the two must be associated. Dissatisfaction in the Christian life is sure to arise if the foundations are ignored. Because men cannot experience the foundations of the Christian faith they are apt to discard them as unnecessary: they are more necessary than all the experiences which spring from them. To say 'You don't need theology to save a soul' is like saying 'What is the good of a foundation? what we want is a house.' The good of the foundation is that when the storms come nothing can wreck the 'house' that is built on the foundation (see Matthew vii. 24–27).

Theology is the science of Christianity; much that is wrongly called theology is mere psychological guess-work, verifiable only from experience. Christian theology is the ordered exposition of revelation certainties. If our teaching and preaching is not based on a recognition of those things that cannot be experienced it will produce parasites, people who depend on being fed by others. We are dealing in these studies with the great fundamental certainties of the Kingdom, and it is essential to take time to soak in these certainties so that when we get out into work we find we are rooted and grounded on the right foundation. If we go into work on the ground of our experience we will soon be exhausted.

What do I know about the foundation truths which I expect to reproduce in my own experience? Experience is an effect; I must have faith in a God whom I never can experience. My experiences are accountable for only by the fact that I am based on God who is bigger than all my experiences of Him. We must take time to know Who it is we worship. We worship a Revelation, not a mystery. "Whom therefore ye ignorantly worship, Him declare I unto you." How can I know God? Jesus Christ has revealed Him: "He that hath seen Me hath seen the Father." I do not *experience* God; I relate all my experiences to the revelation of God which Jesus Christ has made.

II. THE SUPERSTRUCTURE OF CULTIVATION.

"But let every man take heed how he buildeth thereupon." (1 Corinthians iii. 10-15).

Superstructure—anything erected on a foundation.

We are to be "wise masterbuilders," taking care that the superstructure is built according to the foundation, and see to it that we put on the foundation only those things that will stand the fire. Self-interest cannot stand the fire, it is not of the nature of God. There is a danger in us all of ignoring the fundamental things and dealing only with the things that affect our immediate interests; what engrosses our attention actually is what we are after. The 'practical' craze, anything that is efficient, is the insanity of our day—we must be at it! Do anything at all, but don't take time to sit down and think and pray, that is a waste of time; all that is required is to live right practically. If you are living right practically it is because you have not only experienced new birth, but you are being nourished on the right foundation. ". . . and the fire shall try every man's work of what sort it is." We put on the foundation stuff built by our own human energy, consequently as soon as it is touched by the fire of the Presence of God, it fizzles up; it is not of the nature of reality, it does not belong to the foundation. In 1 Corinthians xiii. 1-3, the apostle Paul is referring to the white-heat of emotional energy, the height of intellectual efficiency and competence; I can do certain things and ostensibly prove I can, but, he says, it all amounts to nothing because it is not based on the foundation. The only work that will abide is that which is built on the Foundation, "which is Jesus Christ".

III. THE SUPREMACY OF CHRIST.

"Come unto Me. . . ." (Matthew xi. 28).

Supremacy—highest authority or power.

God never insists on our obedience; human authority does. Our Lord does not give us rules and regulations; He makes very clear what the standard is, and if the relation of my spirit to Him is that of love, I will do all He wants me to do without the slightest hesitation. If I begin to object it is because I love someone else in competition with Him, viz., myself.

Galatians ii. 20 is foundation truth and experimental truth in one—"I am crucified with Christ; nevertheless I live; yet not I, but Christ liveth in me." These words mean the breaking of my independence and surrendering to the supremacy of the Lord Jesus. No one can do this for me, I must do it myself. There is no possibility of debate when once I am there. It is not that we have to do work for God, we have to be so loyal to Jesus Christ that He does His work through us. We learn His truth by obeying it.

"Come unto Me." It is the rarest thing for us to come to Jesus; we come to our own earnestness; we come with notions of what we want. How often have you come to God with your requests and gone away with the feeling, "Oh, well, I have done it this time"! and yet you go away with nothing, while all the time God has stood with out-stretched hands, not only to take you but for you to take Him. Think of the invincible, unconquerable, unwearying patience of Jesus—*"Come unto Me."* The attitude of coming is that you fling yourself entirely on Him, and that is salvation, because *He* is salvation. Stake your all on God, and never be impertinent enough to tell Him that that is what you are doing. *Come*, if you are weary and heavy laden; *ask*, if you are evil; and everything that happens after that is of God.

Printed in the United States
88169LV00004B/338/A